MAD  LIBS®

MORE BEST OF MAD LIBS

By Roger Price and Leonard Stern

Mad Libs
An Imprint of Penguin Random House

MAD LIBS
Penguin Young Readers Group
An Imprint of Penguin Random House LLC

Mad Libs format and text copyright © 2009, 2008, 2007, 2005, 2004, 2003, 2002, 2001,
2000, 1999, 1998, 1997, 1996, 1995, 1994, 1993, 1990, 1989, 1988, 1985, 1982, 1979,
1976, 1970, 1968, 1965, 1959, 1958 by Penguin Random House LLC.
First published in 2009 by Price Stern Sloan. All rights reserved.

Concept created by Roger Price & Leonard Stern

Published by Mad Libs,
an imprint of Penguin Random House LLC,
345 Hudson Street, New York, New York 10014.
Printed in the USA.

ISBN 9780843125498
21 23 25 27 29 30 28 26 24 22

MAD LIBS

INSTRUCTIONS

MAD LIBS® is a game for people who don't like games!
It can be played by one, two, three, four, or forty.

• RIDICULOUSLY SIMPLE DIRECTIONS

In this tablet you will find stories containing blank spaces where words are left out. One player, the READER, selects one of these stories. The READER does not tell anyone what the story is about. Instead, he/she asks the other players, the WRITERS, to give him/her words. These words are used to fill in the blank spaces in the story.

• TO PLAY

The READER asks each WRITER in turn to call out a word—an adjective or a noun or whatever the space calls for—and uses them to fill in the blank spaces in the story. The result is a MAD LIBS® game.

When the READER then reads the completed MAD LIBS® game to the other players, they will discover that they have written a story that is fantastic, screamingly funny, shocking, silly, crazy, or just plain dumb—depending upon which words each WRITER called out.

• EXAMPLE (*Before* and *After*)

"_____!" he said _____
     EXCLAMATION   ADVERB

as he jumped into his convertible _____ and
               NOUN

drove off with his _____ wife.
        ADJECTIVE

"___*Ouch*___!" he said ___*stupidly*___
     EXCLAMATION   ADVERB

as he jumped into his convertible ___*cat*___ and
               NOUN

drove off with his ___*brave*___ wife.
        ADJECTIVE

QUICK REVIEW

In case you have forgotten what adjectives, adverbs, nouns, and verbs are, here is a quick review:

An ADJECTIVE describes something or somebody. *Lumpy, soft, ugly, messy,* and *short* are adjectives.

An ADVERB tells how something is done. It modifies a verb and usually ends in "ly." *Modestly, stupidly, greedily,* and *carefully* are adverbs.

A NOUN is the name of a person, place, or thing. *Sidewalk, umbrella, bridle, bathtub,* and *nose* are nouns.

A VERB is an action word. *Run, pitch, jump,* and *swim* are verbs. Put the verbs in past tense if the directions say PAST TENSE. *Ran, pitched, jumped,* and *swam* are verbs in the past tense.

When we ask for A PLACE, we mean any sort of place: a country or city *(Spain, Cleveland)* or a room *(bathroom, kitchen)*.

An EXCLAMATION or SILLY WORD is any sort of funny sound, gasp, grunt, or outcry, like *Wow!, Ouch!, Whomp!, Ick!,* and *Gadzooks!*

When we ask for specific words, like a NUMBER, a COLOR, an ANIMAL, or a PART OF THE BODY, we mean a word that is one of those things, like *seven, blue, horse,* or *head*.

When we ask for a PLURAL, it means more than one. For example, *cat* pluralized is *cats*.

MAD LIBS® is fun to play with friends, but you can also play it by yourself! To begin with, DO NOT look at the story on the page below. Fill in the blanks on this page with the words called for. Then, using the words you have selected, fill in the blank spaces in the story.

Now you've created your own hilarious MAD LIBS® game!

MAD LIBS

PLURAL NOUN _____

ADJECTIVE _____

PART OF THE BODY _____

NOUN _____

NOUN _____

NOUN _____

NOUN _____

NOUN _____

NOUN _____

NOUN _____

LETTER OF THE ALPHABET _____

LETTER OF THE ALPHABET _____

NOUN _____

PLURAL NOUN _____

NOUN _____

NOUN _____

PART OF THE BODY _____

MAD LIBS®
MAD LIBS

A great word game to play in the car is *Mad* _____. Here are the
                                              PLURAL NOUN

ridiculously _____ instructions. A reader has a *Mad Libs* book
              ADJECTIVE

in one _____ and a pencil or _____ in the
       PART OF THE BODY   NOUN

other. He/She asks each _____ in the car for a part of speech
                         NOUN

(noun, verb, adjective, or _____) to fill in the blanks. In case
                            NOUN

you've forgotten, an adjective is a word used to modify something or some

_____. A noun is the name of a person, _____, or
NOUN   NOUN

_____. A verb is an action _____. An adverb usually
NOUN   NOUN

ends in the letters _____ and _____ and
                    LETTER OF THE ALPHABET   LETTER OF THE ALPHABET

modifies a/an _____. When all the blank _____ are
              NOUN   PLURAL NOUN

filled in, the reader reads the finished _____ aloud. The completed
                                          NOUN

story is usually greeted with shrieks of joy, hoots of _____, and
                                                        NOUN

much _____ clapping.
     PART OF THE BODY

MAD LIBS® is fun to play with friends, but you can also play it by yourself! To begin with, DO NOT look at the story on the page below. Fill in the blanks on this page with the words called for. Then, using the words you have selected, fill in the blank spaces in the story.

Now you've created your own hilarious MAD LIBS® game!

THE OLYMPICS

NOUN _____

PLURAL NOUN _____

ADJECTIVE _____

PLURAL NOUN _____

PLURAL NOUN _____

NUMBER _____

ADJECTIVE _____

ADJECTIVE _____

NOUN _____

ADJECTIVE _____

VERB ENDING IN "S" _____

PART OF THE BODY _____

NOUN _____

ADJECTIVE _____

PLURAL NOUN _____

PLURAL NOUN _____

MAD LIBS®
THE OLYMPICS

Every four years, countries from all over the _____ send their

NOUN

best _____ to compete in _____ games and win

PLURAL NOUN   ADJECTIVE

_____. These events are called the Olympic _____,

PLURAL NOUN   PLURAL NOUN

and they started _____ years ago in _____

NUMBER   ADJECTIVE

Greece. When a winner receives his or her _____ medal at

ADJECTIVE

the games, the national _____ of his or her country is played by

NOUN

a/an _____ band. As the band _____, the citizens

ADJECTIVE   VERB ENDING IN "S"

of that country put their _____ to their chest and join in

PART OF THE BODY

the singing of their national _____. Thanks to television,

NOUN

these _____ events can now be watched by over a billion

ADJECTIVE

_____ throughout the world every four _____.

PLURAL NOUN   PLURAL NOUN

MAD LIBS® is fun to play with friends, but you can also play it by yourself! To begin with, DO NOT look at the story on the page below. Fill in the blanks on this page with the words called for. Then, using the words you have selected, fill in the blank spaces in the story.

Now you've created your own hilarious MAD LIBS® game!

TRUTH OR DARE, PART 1

NOUN _____

PERSON IN ROOM _____

NOUN _____

NUMBER _____

VERB (PAST TENSE) _____

NOUN _____

NUMBER _____

ADJECTIVE _____

VERB _____

NOUN _____

ADJECTIVE _____

NOUN _____

ADJECTIVE _____

TYPE OF LIQUID _____

NOUN _____

PLURAL NOUN _____

TYPE OF LIQUID _____

MAD LIBS®
TRUTH OR DARE, PART 1

Let's play truth or dare! First, some truths:

Q: What is the name of the _____ you like?
NOUN

A: _____
PERSON IN ROOM

Q: What is one _____ no one knows about you?
NOUN

A: When I was _____ years old, I _____ like a/an
NUMBER   VERB (PAST TENSE)

_____ in front of _____ people.
NOUN   NUMBER

Q: If you were stranded on a/an _____ island, what three things
ADJECTIVE

would you bring with you?

A: I couldn't _____ without my precious _____,
VERB   NOUN

my _____ _____, and a/an _____
ADJECTIVE   NOUN   ADJECTIVE

bottle of _____.
TYPE OF LIQUID

Q: What is the strangest _____ you have ever eaten?
NOUN

A: _____ dipped in _____.
PLURAL NOUN   TYPE OF LIQUID

MAD LIBS® is fun to play with friends, but you can also play it by yourself! To begin with, DO NOT look at the story on the page below. Fill in the blanks on this page with the words called for. Then, using the words you have selected, fill in the blank spaces in the story.

Now you've created your own hilarious MAD LIBS® game!

TRUTH OR DARE, PART 2

ADJECTIVE _____

VERB _____

NOUN _____

ADJECTIVE _____

ADJECTIVE _____

NOUN _____

NOUN _____

VERB _____

PLURAL NOUN _____

ADJECTIVE _____

PART OF THE BODY (PLURAL) _____

NUMBER _____

MAD LIBS®
TRUTH OR DARE, PART 2

And now for the dares!

DARE: Pretend you are a/an _____ puppy. _____
                                      ADJECTIVE   VERB

loudly and wag your _____.
                               NOUN

DARE: Put on some _____ music and dance like a/an
                                   ADJECTIVE

_____ _____ for one minute.
ADJECTIVE   NOUN

DARE: Hop on one _____ while you _____ and
                          NOUN   VERB

say the alphabet backward.

DARE: Take off your socks and _____ and step into the shower.
                                 PLURAL NOUN

Then turn on the _____ water and yodel at the top of your
                          ADJECTIVE

_____ for _____ seconds.
PART OF THE BODY (PLURAL)   NUMBER

MAD LIBS® is fun to play with friends, but you can also play it by yourself! To begin with, DO NOT look at the story on the page below. Fill in the blanks on this page with the words called for. Then, using the words you have selected, fill in the blank spaces in the story.

Now you've created your own hilarious MAD LIBS® game!

A VISIT TO THE ZOO

PLURAL NOUN _____

PLURAL NOUN _____

ADJECTIVE _____

TYPE OF LIQUID _____

ANIMAL (PLURAL) _____

ADJECTIVE _____

SILLY WORD _____

SILLY WORD _____

ADJECTIVE _____

PLURAL NOUN _____

ANIMAL _____

ANIMAL _____

PART OF THE BODY _____

PLURAL NOUN _____

ADJECTIVE _____

MAD LIBS®
A VISIT TO THE ZOO

Zoos are places where wild _____ are kept in pens or cages so
            PLURAL NOUN

that _____ can come and look at them. There are two zoos in
        PLURAL NOUN

New York, one in the Bronx and one in _____ Park. The park zoo
                                            ADJECTIVE

is built around a large pond filled with clear sparkling _____. You will
                                                        TYPE OF LIQUID

see several _____ swimming in the pond and eating fish. When it
            ANIMAL (PLURAL)

is feeding time, all of the animals make _____ noises. The elephant
                                            ADJECTIVE

goes "_____" and the turtledoves go "_____."
        SILLY WORD   SILLY WORD

In one part of the zoo, there are _____ gorillas who love
                                        ADJECTIVE

to eat _____. In another building, there is a spotted African
        PLURAL NOUN

_____ that is so fast it can outrun a/an _____.
    ANIMAL   ANIMAL

But my favorite animal is the hippopotamus. It has a huge _____
                                                            PART OF THE BODY

and eats fifty pounds of _____ a day. You would never know that,
                            PLURAL NOUN

technically, it's nothing but an oversized _____ pig.
                                            ADJECTIVE

MAD LIBS® is fun to play with friends, but you can also play it by yourself! To begin with, DO NOT look at the story on the page below. Fill in the blanks on this page with the words called for. Then, using the words you have selected, fill in the blank spaces in the story.

Now you've created your own hilarious MAD LIBS® game!

A BIRTHDAY CARD

PERSON IN ROOM _____

ADJECTIVE _____

NOUN _____

NOUN _____

PLURAL NOUN _____

ADJECTIVE _____

PLURAL NOUN _____

ADJECTIVE _____

NOUN _____

NUMBER _____

PLURAL NOUN _____

NUMBER _____

ADJECTIVE _____

NOUN _____

NOUN _____

PLURAL NOUN _____

PERSON IN ROOM (FEMALE) _____

MAD LIBS®

A BIRTHDAY CARD

Dearest _____,
<u>PERSON IN ROOM</u>

Happy birthday to the most _____ _____ in the
<u>ADJECTIVE</u> <u>NOUN</u>

whole wide _____! I hope all of your _____
<u>NOUN</u> <u>PLURAL NOUN</u>

come true on this _____ day. May your year be filled with
<u>ADJECTIVE</u>

joy and _____. I hope you know how proud I am of what
<u>PLURAL NOUN</u>

a/an _____ young _____ you have become. I
<u>ADJECTIVE</u> <u>NOUN</u>

can hardly believe you're turning _____ years old! My, how
<u>NUMBER</u>

the _____ have flown. I have enclosed a check for
<u>PLURAL NOUN</u>

_____ dollars. I hope you spend it on something that will
<u>NUMBER</u>

make you feel _____. Or perhaps you can put it toward that
<u>ADJECTIVE</u>

newfangled _____ you've been saving for! Happy birthday, my
<u>NOUN</u>

darling _____!
<u>NOUN</u>

Hugs and _____,
<u>PLURAL NOUN</u>

Your Aunt _____
<u>PERSON IN ROOM (FEMALE)</u>

MAD LIBS® is fun to play with friends, but you can also play it by yourself! To begin with, DO NOT look at the story on the page below. Fill in the blanks on this page with the words called for. Then, using the words you have selected, fill in the blank spaces in the story.

Now you've created your own hilarious MAD LIBS® game!

WHOOOOO'S THERE?

ADJECTIVE _____

TYPE OF LIQUID _____

NOUN _____

ADJECTIVE _____

NOUN _____

NOUN _____

ANIMAL _____

NOUN _____

NOUN _____

PLURAL NOUN _____

NOUN _____

NOUN _____

ADJECTIVE _____

NOUN _____

VERB (PAST TENSE) _____

ADJECTIVE _____

NUMBER _____

NOUN _____

MAD LIBS®
WHOOOOO'S THERE?

One night I was sitting alone in my _____ house sipping a cup of
ADJECTIVE

_____ as I read from an old _____. Suddenly, there
TYPE OF LIQUID   NOUN

was a/an _____ noise coming from the _____.
ADJECTIVE   NOUN

The hair on the back of my _____ stood straight up, and I got
NOUN

_____ bumps all over my body. Then I remembered: This
ANIMAL

_____ was supposed to be haunted. Someone or something
NOUN

was down in the _____. I heard clanking _____,
NOUN   PLURAL NOUN

as if a/an _____ were being dragged across the floor of the
NOUN

_____. The room suddenly became _____ and
NOUN   ADJECTIVE

cold. A big white _____ floated right through the door. I nearly
NOUN

_____ in my pants. Speaking in a/an _____ voice,
VERB (PAST TENSE)   ADJECTIVE

the ghost said something I'll never forget if I live to be _____:
NUMBER

"I've just come from the bathroom, and you're out of _____ paper."
NOUN

MAD LIBS® is fun to play with friends, but you can also play it by yourself! To begin with, DO NOT look at the story on the page below. Fill in the blanks on this page with the words called for. Then, using the words you have selected, fill in the blank spaces in the story.

Now you've created your own hilarious MAD LIBS® game!

SAVING GASOLINE

A PLACE _____

PLURAL NOUN _____

ADJECTIVE _____

PLURAL NOUN _____

NOUN _____

ADJECTIVE _____

SILLY WORD _____

TYPE OF LIQUID _____

PLURAL NOUN _____

ADJECTIVE _____

NUMBER _____

NOUN _____

MAD LIBS®
SAVING GASOLINE

Now that Saudi Arabia and (the) _____ have raised the price
                                    A PLACE

of gasoline, millions of patriotic _____ are trying to economize.
                                    PLURAL NOUN

Americans are riding bicycles and _____ small cars. Many people
                                    ADJECTIVE

have turned in their old, gas-guzzling _____ and ride to
                                         PLURAL NOUN

work every day in a/an _____. Scientists are working on
                          NOUN

_____ substitutes for gas. One is called _____.
        ADJECTIVE   SILLY WORD

It is made by mixing regular gasoline with _____. Other
                                             TYPE OF LIQUID

people are depending on electric _____. These are
                                    PLURAL NOUN

very _____. But there is a problem. You have to stop every
        ADJECTIVE

_____ miles to have your _____ recharged!
        NUMBER   NOUN

MAD LIBS® is fun to play with friends, but you can also play it by yourself! To begin with, DO NOT look at the story on the page below. Fill in the blanks on this page with the words called for. Then, using the words you have selected, fill in the blank spaces in the story.

Now you've created your own hilarious MAD LIBS® game!

FOOTBALL BROADCAST

ANIMAL (PLURAL) _____

PLURAL NOUN _____

NOUN _____

CELEBRITY _____

NOUN _____

PART OF THE BODY _____

NUMBER _____

CELEBRITY _____

ADJECTIVE _____

CELEBRITY _____

ADJECTIVE _____

NOUN _____

NOUN _____

VERB ENDING IN "ING" _____

MAD●LIBS®
FOOTBALL BROADCAST

Good afternoon, ladies and gentlemen. This is your favorite sportscaster

bringing you the big football game between the Columbia University

_____ and the West Point _____. The center
　　ANIMAL (PLURAL)　　　　　　　　　　　　　　　　　　PLURAL NOUN

has just snapped the _____ back to the Columbia star halfback,
　　　　　　　　　　　　　　NOUN

_____, who is running around his/her own left _____.
　　CELEBRITY　　　　　　　　　　　　　　　　　　　　　　　　　NOUN

There he/she's tackled hard around the _____. Now it's West
　　　　　　　　　　　　　　　　　　　　　PART OF THE BODY

Point's ball and _____ to go. They're coming out of the huddle.
　　　　　　　　　　NUMBER

The ball is snapped back to _____, who fades back and throws
　　　　　　　　　　　　　　　　　CELEBRITY

a long, _____ pass that is caught by _____, who
　　　　　ADJECTIVE　　　　　　　　　　　　　　　　　　CELEBRITY

is West Point's _____ quarterback. He/She's in the clear, and
　　　　　　　　　　ADJECTIVE

he/she races over the _____ for a touchdown. No, no, wait! The
　　　　　　　　　　　　　NOUN

referee is calling the play back to the thirty-five-_____ line. He's
　　　　　　　　　　　　　　　　　　　　　　　　　　　NOUN

going to penalize West Point for _____.
　　　　　　　　　　　　　　　　　VERB ENDING IN "ING"

MAD LIBS® is fun to play with friends, but you can also play it by yourself! To begin with, DO NOT look at the story on the page below. Fill in the blanks on this page with the words called for. Then, using the words you have selected, fill in the blank spaces in the story.

Now you've created your own hilarious MAD LIBS® game!

LETTER FROM AN AMERICAN IN PARIS

ADJECTIVE _____

PERSON IN ROOM _____

ADJECTIVE _____

ADVERB _____

PLURAL NOUN _____

LAST NAME _____

NOUN _____

SILLY WORD _____

LAST NAME _____

FIRST NAME (FEMALE) _____

SILLY WORD _____

NOUN _____

PLURAL NOUN _____

PLURAL NOUN _____

ADJECTIVE _____

ADJECTIVE _____

NOUN _____

VERB _____

VERB _____

MAD LIBS®

LETTER FROM AN AMERICAN IN PARIS

Dear _____ _____,
      ADJECTIVE   PERSON IN ROOM

I am having a/an _____ time here in Paris. I spend every day
      ADJECTIVE

_____ visiting museums, monuments, and _____.
ADVERB   PLURAL NOUN

Yesterday I went to the _____ Tower, which is located
                             LAST NAME

on the river _____. Then I went to the Jeu de Pomme.
                 NOUN

This is a museum that is spelled J-E-U D-E P-O-M-M-E and is pronounced

_____. It is next to the Louvre, which has the famous
    SILLY WORD

statue of Venus de _____ and the painting of the Mona
               LAST NAME

_____ by Leonardo da _____. The center
FIRST NAME (FEMALE)   SILLY WORD

of Paris is called the Place of the _____ and is always filled
                                  NOUN

with thousands of _____ all taking photographs of one another and
               PLURAL NOUN

of the many French _____. The food at the Paris restaurants is
                 PLURAL NOUN

_____. I have already eaten _____ snails and
ADJECTIVE   ADJECTIVE

duck a la _____. I plan to _____ to Paris
        NOUN   VERB

again next year and hope you can _____, too.
                              VERB

MAD LIBS® is fun to play with friends, but you can also play it by yourself! To begin with, DO NOT look at the story on the page below. Fill in the blanks on this page with the words called for. Then, using the words you have selected, fill in the blank spaces in the story.

Now you've created your own hilarious MAD LIBS® game!

RULES FOR RIDING ON THE SCHOOL BUS

ADJECTIVE _____

NOUN _____

VERB _____

ADJECTIVE _____

NOUN _____

PART OF THE BODY _____

ADJECTIVE _____

TYPE OF CONTAINER _____

PLURAL NOUN _____

VERB _____

NOUN _____

PLURAL NOUN _____

VERB ENDING IN "ING" _____

PLURAL NOUN _____

ADJECTIVE _____

ADVERB _____

ADJECTIVE _____

MAD LIBS®
RULES FOR RIDING ON THE SCHOOL BUS

1. Every morning, your bus runs a/an _____ route, so you must

ADJECTIVE

be sure that you arrive at your local _____ early.

NOUN

2. While waiting, do not _____ in the middle of the street. You

VERB

might get run over by a/an _____ _____.

ADJECTIVE   NOUN

3. When you see the bus, wave your _____.

PART OF THE BODY

4. Before boarding, make sure you have all of your _____ books

ADJECTIVE

and your lunch _____.

TYPE OF CONTAINER

5. When you board the bus, do not push or jostle any of the smaller _____.

PLURAL NOUN

Go to the nearest empty seat and _____.

VERB

6. Do not talk to the _____ while the bus is in motion.

NOUN

7. Do not throw _____ at the other students.

PLURAL NOUN

8. Instead of wasting time by _____, use the trip to study your

VERB ENDING IN "ING"

_____.

PLURAL NOUN

Follow these rules and you will have a/an _____ ride and arrive

ADJECTIVE

_____ at your _____ school.

ADVERB   ADJECTIVE

MAD LIBS® is fun to play with friends, but you can also play it by yourself! To begin with, DO NOT look at the story on the page below. Fill in the blanks on this page with the words called for. Then, using the words you have selected, fill in the blank spaces in the story.

Now you've created your own hilarious MAD LIBS® game!

ES

NUMBER _____

ADJECTIVE _____

PLURAL NOUN _____

ADJECTIVE _____

VERB ENDING IN "ING" _____

ADJECTIVE _____

ADJECTIVE _____

ANIMAL _____

ADJECTIVE _____

NOUN _____

NOUN _____

NOUN _____

PLURAL NOUN _____

ADJECTIVE _____

NOUN _____

ADJECTIVE _____

ADJECTIVE _____

NOUN _____

MAD LIBS®
ES

_ES_, on the air for _____ years, is one of those _____
               NUMBER   ADJECTIVE

programs that has earned both critical _____ and _____
                                          PLURAL NOUN   ADJECTIVE

ratings. Based on the best-_____ book of the same name, this
                      VERB ENDING IN "ING"

_____ drama centers on _____ veterinarians in
   ADJECTIVE   ADJECTIVE

the emergency room of a Chicago cat and _____ hospital. In the
                                              ANIMAL

series, the overworked and _____ vets are the unlikely heroes
                              ADJECTIVE

who make life-and-_____ decisions almost every moment of every
                      NOUN

_____. The series has won seven Golden _____
     NOUN   NOUN

Awards, received a remarkable twenty-one Emmy _____,
                                                  PLURAL NOUN

and has collected seven of those _____ statues. The cast has
                                    ADJECTIVE

won five People's _____ Awards and has been honored four
                     NOUN

_____ years in a row by the Actors Guild of America for a/an
   ADJECTIVE

_____ ensemble performance in a prime-time _____.
   ADJECTIVE   NOUN

MAD LIBS® is fun to play with friends, but you can also play it by yourself! To begin with, DO NOT look at the story on the page below. Fill in the blanks on this page with the words called for. Then, using the words you have selected, fill in the blank spaces in the story.

Now you've created your own hilarious MAD LIBS® game!

PARTY TIME!

ADJECTIVE _____

PLURAL NOUN _____

VERB ENDING IN "ING" _____

PLURAL NOUN _____

CELEBRITY (FEMALE) _____

PERSON IN ROOM (MALE) _____

SILLY WORD _____

VERB _____

TYPE OF FOOD (PLURAL) _____

NOUN _____

SAME TYPE OF FOOD (PLURAL) _____

ADJECTIVE _____

ADJECTIVE _____

PLURAL NOUN _____

NOUN _____

NOUN _____

VERB ENDING IN "ING" _____

NOUN _____

SILLY WORD _____

MAD LIBS®
PARTY TIME!

One of the most _____ things about graduating is that my
                        ADJECTIVE

_____ are _____ a huge party! I decided to have
      PLURAL NOUN   VERB ENDING IN "ING"

a backyard barbecue for all of my family and _____. I've invited
                                                      PLURAL NOUN

my best friends, _____, _____, and of course my
                   CELEBRITY (FEMALE)   PERSON IN ROOM (MALE)

teacher Mrs. _____. My dad is going to _____
                 SILLY WORD   VERB

hamburgers and _____ on his shiny new _____.
                 TYPE OF FOOD (PLURAL)   NOUN

He always thinks his _____ taste really _____,
                      SAME TYPE OF FOOD (PLURAL)   ADJECTIVE

but I think they taste like _____ _____. My mom
                                ADJECTIVE   PLURAL NOUN

is going to make her famous _____ salad, which is my favorite
                                    NOUN

_____ ever! Mom said after we finish _____, we
      NOUN   VERB ENDING IN "ING"

can go swimming in our new _____. _____!
                                    NOUN   SILLY WORD

MAD LIBS® is fun to play with friends, but you can also play it by yourself! To begin with, DO NOT look at the story on the page below. Fill in the blanks on this page with the words called for. Then, using the words you have selected, fill in the blank spaces in the story.

Now you've created your own hilarious MAD LIBS® game!

ROMANTIC MOVIE BLOCKBUSTERS

ADJECTIVE _____

ADJECTIVE _____

PLURAL NOUN _____

NOUN _____

NOUN _____

NOUN _____

PLURAL NOUN _____

A PLACE _____

NOUN _____

VERB _____

NOUN _____

PLURAL NOUN _____

PLURAL NOUN _____

PLURAL NOUN _____

ADJECTIVE _____

MAD LIBS®
ROMANTIC MOVIE BLOCKBUSTERS

Gone With the Wind, set during the _____ War, is the story of Scarlett
                                          ADJECTIVE

O'Hara, a young, _____ -willed woman. She uses her feminine
                      ADJECTIVE

_____ to win back her _____, but in the process
   PLURAL NOUN   NOUN

loses Rhett Butler, the only _____ she ever loved. Most memorable
                                  NOUN

line of dialogue: "Frankly, Scarlett, I don't give a/an _____."
                                                              NOUN

Rick's Café in *Casablanca* is the meeting place for _____ from
                                                         PLURAL NOUN

war-torn (the) _____. Rick sacrifices his love for Ilse when he
                   A PLACE

helps her and her _____ escape the Nazis. Most memorable line:
                       NOUN

"_____ it again, Sam."
    VERB

Love Story is about two _____ -league students. They go
                               NOUN

through all the trials and _____ experienced by all young
                               PLURAL NOUN

_____. Unfortunately, the ending will bring _____
   PLURAL NOUN   PLURAL NOUN

to your eyes. Most memorable line: "Love means never having to say you're

_____."
   ADJECTIVE

MAD LIBS® is fun to play with friends, but you can also play it by yourself! To begin with, DO NOT look at the story on the page below. Fill in the blanks on this page with the words called for. Then, using the words you have selected, fill in the blank spaces in the story.

Now you've created your own hilarious MAD LIBS® game!

BULL FIGHTING

ADJECTIVE _____

A PLACE _____

NOUN _____

SILLY WORD _____

ARTICLE OF CLOTHING _____

SAME ARTICLE OF CLOTHING _____

ADJECTIVE _____

ADJECTIVE _____

PART OF THE BODY _____

SILLY WORD _____

PLURAL NOUN _____

EXCLAMATION _____

ADJECTIVE _____

PLURAL NOUN _____

MAD LIBS®
BULL FIGHTING

Bullfighting is a/an _____ sport which is very popular in (the)
                          ADJECTIVE

_____. A bullfighter is called a *matador*, and his equipment consists
   A PLACE

of a long, sharp _____ called a/an _____, and a
                        NOUN   SILLY WORD

bright red _____. He waves his _____ at the
            ARTICLE OF CLOTHING   SAME ARTICLE OF CLOTHING

bull, which makes the bull _____ and causes him to charge. The
                                ADJECTIVE

matador then goes through a series of _____ maneuvers to avoid
                                            ADJECTIVE

getting caught on the bull's _____. If the matador kills the bull, the
                                PART OF THE BODY

spectators yell, "_____!" and throw their _____
                     SILLY WORD   PLURAL NOUN

into the ring. If the bull wins, they yell "_____!" and call for another
                                              EXCLAMATION

matador. Bullfighting is a very _____ sport, but it will never be popular
                                  ADJECTIVE

in America because Americans don't believe in cruelty to _____.
                                                            PLURAL NOUN

MAD LIBS® is fun to play with friends, but you can also play it by yourself! To begin with, DO NOT look at the story on the page below. Fill in the blanks on this page with the words called for. Then, using the words you have selected, fill in the blank spaces in the story.

Now you've created your own hilarious MAD LIBS® game!

LOOKING GOOD ON PLUTO

NUMBER _____

CITY _____

NOUN _____

ADJECTIVE _____

ADJECTIVE _____

PLURAL NOUN _____

PLURAL NOUN _____

ADJECTIVE _____

TYPE OF LIQUID _____

ARTICLE OF CLOTHING _____

PLURAL NOUN _____

COLOR _____

PART OF THE BODY _____

PART OF THE BODY _____

PLURAL NOUN _____

MAD LIBS®
LOOKING GOOD ON PLUTO

On Pluto, the gravity is _____ times as strong as it is in
NUMBER

_____. So if you are a young _____ there and you
CITY   NOUN

want to look good, here is what you should do. First go to a beauty parlor and

get a/an _____ haircut by a/an _____ Plutonian
         ADJECTIVE   ADJECTIVE

barber. Make sure he keeps your hair out of your _____ so you
                                                  PLURAL NOUN

can show off your _____. This is the _____
                   PLURAL NOUN   ADJECTIVE

fashion on Pluto today. Then spray yourself with _____
                                                  TYPE OF LIQUID

and put on an aluminum foil _____ and high-heeled
                             ARTICLE OF CLOTHING

_____. Makeup is as important on Pluto as it is on Earth, so put
PLURAL NOUN

some bright _____ lipstick on your _____ and
             COLOR   PART OF THE BODY

use a nice _____ shadow. If you follow this advice, you will get
            PART OF THE BODY

your picture on the covers of all their _____.
                                         PLURAL NOUN

MAD LIBS® is fun to play with friends, but you can also play it by yourself! To begin with, DO NOT look at the story on the page below. Fill in the blanks on this page with the words called for. Then, using the words you have selected, fill in the blank spaces in the story.

Now you've created your own hilarious MAD LIBS® game!

START YOUR ENGINES!

NUMBER _____

NOUN _____

PLURAL NOUN _____

ADJECTIVE _____

VERB _____

SILLY WORD _____

FIRST NAME (MALE) _____

SILLY WORD _____

ADJECTIVE _____

ADVERB _____

CELEBRITY (FEMALE) _____

OCCUPATION _____

VERB _____

PLURAL NOUN _____

OCCUPATION _____

MAD LIBS®
START YOUR ENGINES!

There are over _____ ways to look up information on the
               NUMBER

Internet. But before you can get to your favorite website on how to play the

_____ or where to buy _____, you need to have
NOUN   PLURAL NOUN

a/an _____ search engine that will help you _____
     ADJECTIVE   VERB

for the information. My favorite search engine is _____, but
                               SILLY WORD

my friend _____ likes to use _____ instead. He
       FIRST NAME (MALE)   SILLY WORD

says it's faster and more _____. A search engine will help
                   ADJECTIVE

you to find what you are looking for _____ and efficiently. My
                        ADVERB

computer teacher, _____, says a search engine is almost like a/an
         CELEBRITY (FEMALE)

_____ in the sense that it helps you _____ through
OCCUPATION   VERB

a lot of information and helps you find the most important _____. I
                            PLURAL NOUN

knew she was my favorite _____ for a reason!
          OCCUPATION

MAD LIBS® is fun to play with friends, but you can also play it by yourself! To begin with, DO NOT look at the story on the page below. Fill in the blanks on this page with the words called for. Then, using the words you have selected, fill in the blank spaces in the story.

Now you've created your own hilarious MAD LIBS® game!

AND NOW A WORD FROM . . .

ADJECTIVE _____

ADJECTIVE _____

NOUN _____

PLURAL NOUN _____

VERB _____

ADJECTIVE _____

PART OF THE BODY (PLURAL) _____

PLURAL NOUN _____

ADJECTIVE _____

ADJECTIVE _____

NOUN _____

PART OF THE BODY _____

VERB ENDING IN "ING" _____

PLURAL NOUN _____

MAD LIBS®
AND NOW A WORD FROM . . .

It is almost impossible to watch _____-time television without having
ADJECTIVE

some _____ athlete pitching a/an _____ for you to buy. They
ADJECTIVE   NOUN

sell you everything from soup to _____. They are spokespersons
PLURAL NOUN

for sneakers that _____, as well as _____-smelling
VERB   ADJECTIVE

deodorants you put under your _____. Other products
PART OF THE BODY (PLURAL)

they endorse are designer _____, watches with _____
PLURAL NOUN   ADJECTIVE

movements, and _____ razors, which they guarantee will remove
ADJECTIVE

every _____ from your _____. Athletes make more
NOUN   PART OF THE BODY

money from _____ products than they can earn from playing
VERB ENDING IN "ING"

_____.
PLURAL NOUN

MAD LIBS® is fun to play with friends, but you can also play it by yourself! To begin with, DO NOT look at the story on the page below. Fill in the blanks on this page with the words called for. Then, using the words you have selected, fill in the blank spaces in the story.

Now you've created your own hilarious MAD LIBS® game!

ADVICE COLUMN

PERSON IN ROOM (FIRST NAME) _____

ADJECTIVE _____

NOUN _____

NOUN _____

PLURAL NOUN _____

VERB ENDING IN "ING" _____

NOUN _____

NUMBER _____

SAME PERSON IN ROOM (FIRST NAME) _____

NOUN _____

ADJECTIVE _____

PLURAL NOUN _____

NOUN _____

ADVERB _____

NOUN _____

NOUN _____

NOUN _____

VERB _____

ADJECTIVE _____

NOUN _____

NOUN _____

MAD LIBS®
ADVICE COLUMN

Dear _____, My _____ daughter wants
　　　　PERSON IN ROOM (FIRST NAME)　　　　　　ADJECTIVE

to wear a mini _____ with a bare _____. She claims
　　　　　　　　NOUN　　　　　　　　　　　　NOUN

all the other _____ her age are _____ them.
　　　　　　　PLURAL NOUN　　　　　　　　VERB ENDING IN "ING"

What to do? Signed, An Anxious _____
　　　　　　　　　　　　　　　　NOUN

Dear Anxious, Take my advice: Ground your daughter for _____ days.
　　　　　　　　　　　　　　　　　　　　　　　　　　　NUMBER

Dear _____, My oldest _____ is
　　　SAME PERSON IN ROOM (FIRST NAME)　　　　　　NOUN

a/an _____ slob. As often as I try, I can never get him to brush his
　　　ADJECTIVE

_____, or comb his _____ before going to school. He
　PLURAL NOUN　　　　　　　　NOUN

also _____ refuses to take a bath or a/an _____, clean
　　　ADVERB　　　　　　　　　　　　　　　　　NOUN

up his _____, or make up the very _____ he sleeps in.
　　　NOUN　　　　　　　　　　　　　　　NOUN

How can I _____? Signed, A/An _____ Mother
　　　　　VERB　　　　　　　　　　　ADJECTIVE

Dear Mother, You better clean that _____ up before he turns into
　　　　　　　　　　　　　　　　NOUN

a filthy ball of _____.
　　　　　　　　NOUN

MAD LIBS® is fun to play with friends, but you can also play it by yourself! To begin with, DO NOT look at the story on the page below. Fill in the blanks on this page with the words called for. Then, using the words you have selected, fill in the blank spaces in the story.

Now you've created your own hilarious MAD LIBS® game!

SAFETY PRECAUTIONS FOR CAMPERS

NOUN _____

ADJECTIVE _____

ADJECTIVE _____

SILLY WORD _____

NOUN _____

NOUN _____

TYPE OF LIQUID _____

ANIMAL _____

EXCLAMATION _____

NUMBER _____

PLURAL NOUN _____

NOUN _____

A PLACE _____

TYPE OF FOOD (PLURAL) _____

NOUN _____

ADVERB _____

MAD◯LIBS®
SAFETY PRECAUTIONS FOR CAMPERS

Attention, all campers! Just a few weeks ago you were a miserable

_____, living in the _____ city with your
   NOUN   ADJECTIVE

_____ parents. But a few weeks at Camp _____ will
   ADJECTIVE   SILLY WORD

turn you into a self-reliant, fearless _____. But, you must learn to
                                              NOUN

exist in the wild.

Rule One: If you catch a/an _____ and make a fire to cook it,
                                    NOUN

always remember to pour _____ on the fire when you're through.
                              TYPE OF LIQUID

Smokey the _____ always says, "_____!"
                 ANIMAL   EXCLAMATION

Rule Two: Do not go more than _____ yards away from the trail.
                                       NUMBER

If you get lost, remember that _____ always grow on the north
                                       PLURAL NOUN

side of a/an _____. If you have a compass, the needle will always
                   NOUN

point toward (the) _____. If you run into a bear, do not give it
                          A PLACE

_____. Just be calm and climb a/an _____.
   TYPE OF FOOD (PLURAL)   NOUN

If you follow these rules, you can live very _____ in the woods.
                                                    ADVERB

The stories in this book were originally published between 1958 and 2009 by Price Stern Sloan.
Copyright © Penguin Random House LLC.

MAD LIBS® is fun to play with friends, but you can also play it by yourself! To begin with, DO NOT look at the story on the page below. Fill in the blanks on this page with the words called for. Then, using the words you have selected, fill in the blank spaces in the story.

Now you've created your own hilarious MAD LIBS® game!

SCOOP!

ADJECTIVE _____

VERB _____

PLURAL NOUN _____

ADJECTIVE _____

VERB _____

OCCUPATION _____

ADJECTIVE _____

PLURAL NOUN _____

A PLACE _____

ADJECTIVE _____

CITY _____

SILLY WORD _____

ADJECTIVE _____

OCCUPATION (PLURAL) _____

ADJECTIVE _____

VERB _____

MAD LIBS®
SCOOP!

There is nothing better than joining a/an _____ club or activity after
ADJECTIVE

school. It's a great way to _____, meet new _____,
VERB   PLURAL NOUN

and all your teachers will think you are really _____. My favorite
ADJECTIVE

activity is the school newspaper. We _____ and write articles.
VERB

Once, I even got to interview a/an _____, and another time I
OCCUPATION

wrote a/an _____ article about the _____ they serve
ADJECTIVE   PLURAL NOUN

in the school _____. I think when I am _____ that
A PLACE   ADJECTIVE

I would like to be an investigative reporter for the _____ *Times*,
CITY

or for some famous TV show—just like Barbara _____. She's just
SILLY WORD

_____. She gets to meet all sorts of famous _____,
ADJECTIVE   OCCUPATION (PLURAL)

ask them _____ questions, and make them _____.
ADJECTIVE   VERB

What a great job!

MAD LIBS® is fun to play with friends, but you can also play it by yourself! To begin with, DO NOT look at the story on the page below. Fill in the blanks on this page with the words called for. Then, using the words you have selected, fill in the blank spaces in the story.

Now you've created your own hilarious MAD LIBS® game!

LETTER TO
A FAMOUS SCARY GUY

LAST NAME _____

NOUN _____

ADJECTIVE _____

ADJECTIVE _____

ANIMAL (PLURAL) _____

A PLACE _____

ANIMAL _____

ADJECTIVE _____

SILLY WORD _____

PLURAL NOUN _____

ARTICLE OF CLOTHING _____

PERSON IN ROOM _____

NUMBER _____

ADJECTIVE _____

VERB ENDING IN "ING" _____

ADJECTIVE _____

PERSON IN ROOM (MALE) _____

MAD LIBS®
LETTER TO A FAMOUS SCARY GUY

Dear Mr. _____,
              LAST NAME

You are my favorite Hollywood _____ because you have done so
                                  NOUN

many _____ horror films. I loved you in *The* _____
       ADJECTIVE   ADJECTIVE

Museum and *The* _____ *from (the)* _____ and *The*
                ANIMAL (PLURAL)   A PLACE

Night the Vampires Met and _____ *Man.* My particular favorite
                             ANIMAL

was the _____ role you played in *Doctor* _____
           ADJECTIVE   SILLY WORD

and the Yucky, Slimy, Really Horrible _____. You wore
                                PLURAL NOUN

a long white _____ and had a beard that made you look
         ARTICLE OF CLOTHING

like _____. I saw that _____ times. You are
    PERSON IN ROOM   NUMBER

a/an _____ good actor and should get the Academy Award for
      ADJECTIVE

_____. I think you are almost as scary as my other favorite
VERB ENDING IN "ING"

_____ actor, _____ Mouse.
  ADJECTIVE   PERSON IN ROOM (MALE)

MAD LIBS® is fun to play with friends, but you can also play it by yourself! To begin with, DO NOT look at the story on the page below. Fill in the blanks on this page with the words called for. Then, using the words you have selected, fill in the blank spaces in the story.

Now you've created your own hilarious MAD LIBS® game!

THE BAKERY

ADJECTIVE _____

NOUN _____

PLURAL NOUN _____

PLURAL NOUN _____

NOUN _____

NUMBER _____

TYPE OF FOOD (PLURAL) _____

NOUN _____

NUMBER _____

PLURAL NOUN _____

NUMBER _____

PLURAL NOUN _____

COLOR _____

NOUN _____

MAD LIBS®
THE BAKERY

CLERK: Good day, miss. What can I do for you?

CUSTOMER: I want to buy some _____ bread.
         ADJECTIVE

CLERK: Do you want a loaf of whole-grain _____ or would you like
                                          NOUN

some buttermilk _____?
         PLURAL NOUN

CUSTOMER: Just a regular loaf with sesame _____ on it.
                                            PLURAL NOUN

CLERK: All right now, how about some nice _____ cake?
                                            NOUN

CUSTOMER: Well, I have _____ children, and they all like to eat
                         NUMBER

sweet _____. How much are your cookies?
      TYPE OF FOOD (PLURAL)

CLERK: We have _____-chip cookies at _____ dollars a pound.
                NOUN   NUMBER

And we have this box of assorted little _____ for only two dollars.
                                         PLURAL NOUN

CUSTOMER: I'll take one. They look like they don't have more than

_____ calories.
   NUMBER

CLERK: All right. That will be one box of _____, our special
                                           PLURAL NOUN

_____ berry pie, and a big family-sized loaf of _____.
   COLOR   NOUN

MAD LIBS® is fun to play with friends, but you can also play it by yourself! To begin with, DO NOT look at the story on the page below. Fill in the blanks on this page with the words called for. Then, using the words you have selected, fill in the blank spaces in the story.

Now you've created your own hilarious MAD LIBS® game!

SNOWMAN-BUILDING

ADJECTIVE _____

NOUN _____

NOUN _____

ADJECTIVE _____

NOUN _____

ADJECTIVE _____

PLURAL NOUN _____

PART OF THE BODY (PLURAL) _____

NOUN _____

COLOR _____

NOUN _____

PLURAL NOUN _____

ADJECTIVE _____

NOUN _____

NOUN _____

ADJECTIVE _____

NOUN _____

NOUN _____

MAD LIBS®
SNOWMAN-BUILDING

Question: What kid hasn't loved the _____ thrill of building a/an
                                        ADJECTIVE

_____ man?
NOUN

Answer: Kids who live where the _____ never stops shining.
                                     NOUN

Nevertheless, snowman-building is one of the most _____
                                                   ADJECTIVE

competitions at the winter games. Each team is given several hundred pounds

of powdered _____ to mold and shape into what they hope will be
             NOUN

the most _____ snowman anyone has ever laid _____
          ADJECTIVE   PLURAL NOUN

on. This year's winner was so adorable that everyone wanted to throw their

_____ around him and hug his _____. They
PART OF THE BODY (PLURAL)   NOUN

used a bright _____ _____ for his nose, two shiny
               COLOR   NOUN

_____ for his eyes, and a/an _____ _____
PLURAL NOUN   ADJECTIVE   NOUN

on his head for a hat. In addition, they put a corncob _____ in his
                                                        NOUN

mouth and tied a/an _____ scarf around his neck. Their prizewinning
                     ADJECTIVE

_____ quickly became the talk of the _____.
NOUN   NOUN

MAD LIBS® is fun to play with friends, but you can also play it by yourself! To begin with, DO NOT look at the story on the page below. Fill in the blanks on this page with the words called for. Then, using the words you have selected, fill in the blank spaces in the story.

Now you've created your own hilarious MAD LIBS® game!

OUR FAVORITE RESTAURANT

NOUN _____

NOUN _____

ADJECTIVE _____

NOUN _____

NOUN _____

PLURAL NOUN _____

PLURAL NOUN _____

NOUN _____

ADJECTIVE _____

PLURAL NOUN _____

PLURAL NOUN _____

PLURAL NOUN _____

NOUN _____

NOUN _____

ADJECTIVE _____

NOUN _____

ADJECTIVE _____

NOUN _____

MAD LIBS®
OUR FAVORITE RESTAURANT

Our family's favorite eating _____ is the Shanghai _____.
NOUN   NOUN

Dad loves it because it's a/an _____ walk from our house and
ADJECTIVE

he doesn't have to drive the _____ guzzler. We love it because
NOUN

the Chinese food is out of this _____. We always order the same
NOUN

_____—steamed _____, minced _____ in
PLURAL NOUN   PLURAL NOUN   NOUN

lettuce cups, sweet-and-_____ barbecued _____, and a
ADJECTIVE   PLURAL NOUN

bowl of fried _____. Then comes the best part of the meal—fortune
PLURAL NOUN

_____! I always save my fortunes. My current favorites are:
PLURAL NOUN

1. You will receive an important _____ from a mysterious
NOUN

_____.
NOUN

2. As the sun rises, a/an _____ opportunity will present itself . . . be
ADJECTIVE

sure to take advantage of it before the _____ goes down.
NOUN

3. Tomorrow you will be called upon to make a/an _____
ADJECTIVE

decision that will affect the rest of your _____.
NOUN

MAD LIBS® is fun to play with friends, but you can also play it by yourself! To begin with, DO NOT look at the story on the page below. Fill in the blanks on this page with the words called for. Then, using the words you have selected, fill in the blank spaces in the story.

Now you've created your own hilarious MAD LIBS® game!

WORD GAMES

PLURAL NOUN _____

NOUN _____

NOUN _____

ADJECTIVE _____

PLURAL NOUN _____

PLURAL NOUN _____

NOUN _____

PLURAL NOUN _____

VERB _____

ADJECTIVE _____

ADJECTIVE _____

SAME ADJECTIVE _____

VERB _____

VERB ENDING IN "ING" _____

SAME ADJECTIVE _____

PLURAL NOUN _____

MAD LIBS®
WORD GAMES

In the early 1900s, crossword _____ only appeared in children's
                                    PLURAL NOUN

books. Today, _____ puzzles are in almost every _____
                   NOUN   NOUN

printed in the United States and throughout the whole _____
                                                            ADJECTIVE

world. More people do crossword puzzles than smoke _____ or
                                                          PLURAL NOUN

drink _____. Some fanatics are known to do their puzzles even
          PLURAL NOUN

before they wash their _____, brush their _____,
                              NOUN   PLURAL NOUN

or _____ their breakfast. Another _____ word
         VERB   ADJECTIVE

game is _____ Libs. Not only is _____ Libs fun to
              ADJECTIVE   SAME ADJECTIVE

_____, but it is also an informative _____ tool. By
       VERB   VERB ENDING IN "ING"

playing _____ Libs, kids learn how to use nouns, adjectives, adverbs,
              SAME ADJECTIVE

and _____.
         PLURAL NOUN

MAD LIBS® is fun to play with friends, but you can also play it by yourself! To begin with, DO NOT look at the story on the page below. Fill in the blanks on this page with the words called for. Then, using the words you have selected, fill in the blank spaces in the story.

Now you've created your own hilarious MAD LIBS® game!

AN ART NAMED MARTIAL

PLURAL NOUN _____

ADJECTIVE _____

PERSON IN ROOM _____

ADJECTIVE _____

NOUN _____

ADJECTIVE _____

PLURAL NOUN _____

ANIMAL _____

VERB _____

NOUN _____

NOUN _____

PART OF THE BODY _____

NOUN _____

NOUN _____

PART OF THE BODY (PLURAL) _____

MAD LIBS®
AN ART NAMED MARTIAL

Want to become an expert in karate or kung fu? You can learn martial

_____ in three _____ lessons with Master
    PLURAL NOUN   ADJECTIVE

_____'s videotape. This _____-selling tape takes you
PERSON IN ROOM   ADJECTIVE

step-by-_____ through a series of _____ exercises
          NOUN   ADJECTIVE

guaranteed to develop _____ in your body and make you strong as
                PLURAL NOUN

a/an _____. In less than a week, you will be able to do one hundred
      ANIMAL

_____-ups a day, skip a jumping _____ for an hour,
       VERB   NOUN

and climb a/an _____ without losing your _____.
           NOUN   PART OF THE BODY

And believe it or not, by the end of the month, you'll not only be eligible for

a black _____, but be capable of breaking a four-inch-thick
           NOUN

_____ easily with your own two _____!
    NOUN   PART OF THE BODY (PLURAL)

MAD LIBS® is fun to play with friends, but you can also play it by yourself! To begin with, DO NOT look at the story on the page below. Fill in the blanks on this page with the words called for. Then, using the words you have selected, fill in the blank spaces in the story.

Now you've created your own hilarious MAD LIBS® game!

LOVE SCENE

PERSON IN ROOM (FEMALE) _____

PERSON IN ROOM (MALE) _____

ADJECTIVE _____

ADJECTIVE _____

PLURAL NOUN _____

NOUN _____

ADJECTIVE _____

NOUN _____

NOUN _____

VERB ENDING IN "ING" _____

NOUN _____

NOUN _____

NOUN _____

CELEBRITY _____

MAD LIBS®
LOVE SCENE

To be performed by _____ *and* _____.
PERSON IN ROOM (FEMALE)　　　　　PERSON IN ROOM (MALE)

GIRL: Before I go inside, I want to thank you for a/an _____ evening.
ADJECTIVE

I've really had a/an _____ time.
ADJECTIVE

BOY: I'll bet you tell that to all the _____.
PLURAL NOUN

GIRL: You'd better go now before my _____ hears you and wakes
NOUN

up. He's a very _____ sleeper.
ADJECTIVE

BOY: I don't care. Darling, I love you more than _____ itself. Let me
NOUN

take you away from this terrible _____.
NOUN

GIRL: You've got to be _____. I wouldn't run away with you if
VERB ENDING IN "ING"

you were the last _____ on earth.
NOUN

BOY: But darling, you're breaking my _____. I love you. Please
NOUN

marry me and be my _____.
NOUN

GIRL: I'm sorry, but I'm already engaged to _____.
CELEBRITY

MAD LIBS® is fun to play with friends, but you can also play it by yourself! To begin with, DO NOT look at the story on the page below. Fill in the blanks on this page with the words called for. Then, using the words you have selected, fill in the blank spaces in the story.

Now you've created your own hilarious MAD LIBS® game!

PIRATE MOVIES

PLURAL NOUN _____

PLURAL NOUN _____

NOUN _____

PLURAL NOUN _____

PLURAL NOUN _____

NOUN _____

PLURAL NOUN _____

NOUN _____

PLURAL NOUN _____

ADJECTIVE _____

NOUN _____

NOUN _____

PLURAL NOUN _____

ADJECTIVE _____

PLURAL NOUN _____

CELEBRITY (MALE) _____

ADJECTIVE _____

PERSON IN ROOM _____

PART OF THE BODY _____

ADJECTIVE _____

NOUN _____

MAD LIBS®
PIRATE MOVIES

Even in the days of silent _____, pirate movies were smash
<u>PLURAL NOUN</u>

_____ at the box _____, earning millions of
<u>PLURAL NOUN</u>   <u>NOUN</u>

_____. They enchanted kids and _____ alike.
<u>PLURAL NOUN</u>   <u>PLURAL NOUN</u>

But in real life, pirates were as different from the ones on film as night and

_____. They were ruthless and cold-blooded _____
<u>NOUN</u>   <u>PLURAL NOUN</u>

who had no respect for law and _____. Movies made pirates seem
<u>NOUN</u>

as lovable as teddy _____. In the 1920s in the _____
<u>PLURAL NOUN</u>   <u>ADJECTIVE</u>

silent film "_____," Douglas Fairbanks played the first swashbuckling
<u>NOUN</u>

_____ to ever roam the seven _____ in search
<u>NOUN</u>   <u>PLURAL NOUN</u>

of _____ adventures and _____ in distress. Today,
<u>ADJECTIVE</u>   <u>PLURAL NOUN</u>

_____ carries on this _____ tradition with his
<u>CELEBRITY (MALE)</u>   <u>ADJECTIVE</u>

portrayal of _____ Sparrow, a tongue-in-_____ pirate
<u>PERSON IN ROOM</u>   <u>PART OF THE BODY</u>

buccaneer. Throughout the years, pirates have had a/an _____
<u>ADJECTIVE</u>

way of lighting up the silver _____!
<u>NOUN</u>

MAD LIBS® is fun to play with friends, but you can also play it by yourself! To begin with, DO NOT look at the story on the page below. Fill in the blanks on this page with the words called for. Then, using the words you have selected, fill in the blank spaces in the story.

Now you've created your own hilarious MAD LIBS® game!

ADVICE TO PROSPECTIVE PARENTS

ADJECTIVE _____

ADJECTIVE _____

NOUN _____

NOUN _____

NOUN _____

ADJECTIVE _____

NOUN _____

ADJECTIVE _____

PLURAL NOUN _____

NUMBER _____

PLURAL NOUN _____

ADVERB _____

NOUN _____

EXCLAMATION _____

NOUN _____

MAD LIBS®
ADVICE TO PROSPECTIVE PARENTS

Congratulations to all of you _____ mothers and _____
 ADJECTIVE ADJECTIVE

fathers. You are about to give birth to a/an _____. Remember,
 NOUN

a happy child comes from a happy _____. The arrival of your
 NOUN

_____ will cause many _____ changes in your life.
NOUN ADJECTIVE

You'll probably have to get up at four A.M. to give the little _____
 NOUN

its bottle of _____ milk and change his or her _____.
 ADJECTIVE PLURAL NOUN

Later, when he or she is _____ years old and able to walk, you'll hear
 NUMBER

the patter of little _____ around the house. And in no time, your child
 PLURAL NOUN

will be talking _____, and calling you his or her "_____,"
 ADVERB NOUN

and saying things like, "_____!" right to your face. It's no wonder
 EXCLAMATION

they are called little bundles of _____.
 NOUN

MAD LIBS® is fun to play with friends, but you can also play it by yourself! To begin with, DO NOT look at the story on the page below. Fill in the blanks on this page with the words called for. Then, using the words you have selected, fill in the blank spaces in the story.

Now you've created your own hilarious MAD LIBS® game!

GEOGRAPHY, PART 1

ADJECTIVE _____

ADJECTIVE _____

PLURAL NOUN _____

ADJECTIVE _____

PLURAL NOUN _____

PLURAL NOUN _____

PLURAL NOUN _____

PLURAL NOUN _____

PLURAL NOUN _____

VERB ENDING IN "ING" _____

A PLACE _____

A PLACE _____

ADJECTIVE _____

NOUN _____

ADVERB _____

ADVERB _____

MAD○LIBS®
GEOGRAPHY, PART 1

_____ experts have taken many _____ polls that
    ADJECTIVE   ADJECTIVE

indicate that most American _____ who attend the average
                           PLURAL NOUN

American _____ school don't know anything about geography.
           ADJECTIVE

These _____ don't know much about _____ or
      PLURAL NOUN   PLURAL NOUN

_____ either, but geography is important because it teaches us
  PLURAL NOUN

where all the continents, countries, states, and _____ are. Geography
                                   PLURAL NOUN

also helps us learn the capitals of all the _____ and is just as
                               PLURAL NOUN

important as math or English or _____. Besides, if you don't know
                      VERB ENDING IN "ING"

anything about geography, you might start traveling to (the) _____
                                          A PLACE

from Fort Worth, Texas, and end up in (the) _____. Or maybe you'd
                              A PLACE

end up in a really _____ place like New _____ City. So
           ADJECTIVE   NOUN

the next time you have geography class, listen _____ to your
                                  ADVERB

teacher and study _____.
       ADVERB

MAD LIBS® is fun to play with friends, but you can also play it by yourself! To begin with, DO NOT look at the story on the page below. Fill in the blanks on this page with the words called for. Then, using the words you have selected, fill in the blank spaces in the story.

Now you've created your own hilarious MAD LIBS® game!

GEOGRAPHY, PART 2

ADJECTIVE _____

TYPE OF LIQUID _____

NOUN _____

PLURAL NOUN _____

ADJECTIVE _____

A PLACE _____

A PLACE _____

SILLY WORD _____

A PLACE _____

NOUN _____

A PLACE _____

NUMBER _____

A PLACE_____

MAD LIBS®
GEOGRAPHY, PART 2

Here are some _____ geographical facts that you should know.
ADJECTIVE

A peninsula is an area of land surrounded by _____ and
TYPE OF LIQUID

connected to the mainland by a/an _____.
NOUN

Texas has more _____ and more _____ cows than
PLURAL NOUN   ADJECTIVE

(the) _____.
A PLACE

The capital of (the) _____ is _____.
A PLACE   SILLY WORD

The Grand Canyon in (the) _____ is the largest _____
A PLACE   NOUN

in the world.

The Mississippi River runs from (the) _____ through _____
A PLACE   NUMBER

states and winds up in the Gulf of (the) _____.
A PLACE

MAD LIBS® is fun to play with friends, but you can also play it by yourself! To begin with, DO NOT look at the story on the page below. Fill in the blanks on this page with the words called for. Then, using the words you have selected, fill in the blank spaces in the story.

Now you've created your own hilarious MAD LIBS® game!

DR. JEKYLL AND MR. HYDE, LTD.

NOUN _____

PLURAL NOUN _____

ADJECTIVE _____

ADJECTIVE _____

CITY _____

ADJECTIVE _____

NOUN _____

ADJECTIVE _____

PERSON IN ROOM _____

ADJECTIVE _____

PLURAL NOUN _____

NOUN _____

NOUN _____

ADJECTIVE _____

TYPE OF LIQUID _____

NOUN _____

NOUN _____

ADJECTIVE _____

PLURAL NOUN _____

MAD LIBS®
DR. JEKYLL AND MR. HYDE, LTD.

This scary _____ was written over 100 _____
             NOUN   PLURAL NOUN

ago and made its author very _____. The story is about a/an
                                   ADJECTIVE

_____ doctor in _____ who performs _____
   ADJECTIVE   CITY   ADJECTIVE

experiments in his science _____ to see if he can change his
                                  NOUN

personality. He succeeds, and turns himself into a/an _____
                                                            ADJECTIVE

monster he calls Mr. _____. The monster is very
                        PERSON IN ROOM

_____ and _____ are terrified of him. The
   ADJECTIVE   PLURAL NOUN

police begin a/an _____-hunt for him and put out an all-points
                        NOUN

_____. After a tip from a/an _____ neighbor, they
   NOUN   ADJECTIVE

find him in Dr. Jekyll's lab trying to drink a bottle of _____ so
                                                          TYPE OF LIQUID

he can change back to his original _____. Unfortunately, it's too
                                        NOUN

late, and both Dr. Jekyll and Mr. Hyde meet an untimely _____.
                                                              NOUN

The moral of this _____ story is: Beware of people with split
                       ADJECTIVE

_____.
   PLURAL NOUN

MAD LIBS® is fun to play with friends, but you can also play it by yourself! To begin with, DO NOT look at the story on the page below. Fill in the blanks on this page with the words called for. Then, using the words you have selected, fill in the blank spaces in the story.

Now you've created your own hilarious MAD LIBS® game!

THE AMAZING RANDY

PLURAL NOUN _____

NOUN _____

NOUN _____

NOUN _____

ANIMAL _____

NOUN _____

NOUN _____

ADJECTIVE _____

NOUN _____

ADJECTIVE _____

TYPE OF LIQUID _____

TYPE OF LIQUID _____

ADJECTIVE _____

NOUN _____

SILLY WORD _____

MAD LIBS®
THE AMAZING RANDY

Recently on TV, I saw an amazing magician and escape artist. Both of his

_____ were laced up in a straitjacket, and he was suspended by
  PLURAL NOUN

a/an _____ sixty feet in the air over a busy _____.
       NOUN   NOUN

And he escaped! A man who can do that must be a real _____.
                                                           NOUN

I saw a magician once who put a/an _____ in a/an _____
                                        ANIMAL   NOUN

and then waved his magic _____ and made it disappear.
                              NOUN

I saw another _____ magician who sawed a beautiful
                    ADJECTIVE

_____ in half right on the stage. If you practice hard, there are
    NOUN

several _____ magic tricks you can learn to do. For instance,
           ADJECTIVE

you can learn how to take a glass of _____ and turn it into
                                       TYPE OF LIQUID

_____. Or you can wave a/an _____ wand in
 TYPE OF LIQUID   ADJECTIVE

the air and make it turn into a red _____. All you have to do is
                                         NOUN

memorize the secret magic word, "_____."
                                    SILLY WORD

MAD LIBS® is fun to play with friends, but you can also play it by yourself! To begin with, DO NOT look at the story on the page below. Fill in the blanks on this page with the words called for. Then, using the words you have selected, fill in the blank spaces in the story.

Now you've created your own hilarious MAD LIBS® game!

OUR SCHOOL

SCHOOL _____

ADJECTIVE _____

ADJECTIVE _____

NUMBER _____

NUMBER _____

PLURAL NOUN _____

SAME PLURAL NOUN _____

ADJECTIVE _____

PLURAL NOUN _____

NOUN _____

TYPE OF LIQUID _____

CELEBRITY _____

NOUN _____

NOUN _____

ADJECTIVE _____

MAD LIBS®
OUR SCHOOL

_____ is one of America's most _____

SCHOOL ADJECTIVE

institutions of _____ learning. The student body is composed of

ADJECTIVE

_____ males and _____ _____.

NUMBER NUMBER PLURAL NOUN

The _____ get the best grades. Students can eat lunch

SAME PLURAL NOUN

in the _____ school cafeteria, which features boiled

ADJECTIVE

_____ and _____ sandwiches, with

PLURAL NOUN NOUN

all the _____ they can drink, for only seventy-four cents. The

TYPE OF LIQUID

principal of the school, _____, is raising money to build a new

CELEBRITY

_____ laboratory and a new football _____. Any

NOUN NOUN

student who goes to this school can consider himself very _____.

ADJECTIVE

MAD LIBS® is fun to play with friends, but you can also play it by yourself! To begin with, DO NOT look at the story on the page below. Fill in the blanks on this page with the words called for. Then, using the words you have selected, fill in the blank spaces in the story.

Now you've created your own hilarious MAD LIBS® game!

COLUMBUS AND ISABELLA

A PLACE _____

PLURAL NOUN _____

PLURAL NOUN _____

ADJECTIVE _____

PLURAL NOUN _____

NOUN _____

EXCLAMATION _____

PERSON IN ROOM (MALE) _____

PLURAL NOUN _____

TYPE OF LIQUID _____

PLURAL NOUN _____

ADJECTIVE _____

NOUN _____

MAD LIBS®
COLUMBUS AND ISABELLA

A dramatic scene:

COLUMBUS: Queen Isabella, it is I, Christopher Columbus. I have returned after

discovering a new route to (the) _____
                                    A PLACE

ISABELLA: That's news, Columbus. Did you bring back lots of silver and precious

_____?
   PLURAL NOUN

COLUMBUS: No, your majesty. But you will never have to pawn the royal

_____ again. I discovered a/an _____ land
      PLURAL NOUN   ADJECTIVE

populated by fierce _____, and I claimed them all in the name of
                         PLURAL NOUN

the Spanish _____.
                 NOUN

ISABELLA: _____! This will please my husband, _____.
              EXCLAMATION   PERSON IN ROOM (MALE)

What are these natives called?

COLUMBUS: They are called _____, your majesty. They put
                                PLURAL NOUN

_____ on their faces and wear _____ in their hair.
   TYPE OF LIQUID   PLURAL NOUN

ISABELLA: You have made a/an _____ voyage, Columbus, and your
                                    ADJECTIVE

_____ will go down in history!
      NOUN

MAD LIBS® is fun to play with friends, but you can also play it by yourself! To begin with, DO NOT look at the story on the page below. Fill in the blanks on this page with the words called for. Then, using the words you have selected, fill in the blank spaces in the story.

Now you've created your own hilarious MAD LIBS® game!

GIRL BAND

ADJECTIVE _____

PERSON IN ROOM (FEMALE) _____

NOUN _____

PERSON IN ROOM (FEMALE) _____

ADJECTIVE _____

NOUN _____

NUMBER _____

NOUN _____

ADVERB _____

ADVERB _____

ADJECTIVE _____

PLURAL NOUN _____

NUMBER _____

SILLY WORD _____

NUMBER _____

ADJECTIVE _____

MAD LIBS®
GIRL BAND

After school this year, my friends and I decided that we should start a/an

_____ all-girl band. I have a piano, _____ plays
ADJECTIVE   PERSON IN ROOM (FEMALE)

the _____, _____ plays the _____
        NOUN   PERSON IN ROOM (FEMALE)   ADJECTIVE

drums, and Christine has been taking lessons on the _____
                                                              NOUN

since she was _____ years old! Our first rehearsal was a/an
                    NUMBER

_____.We couldn't believe how _____ we played!
     NOUN   ADVERB

But we all went home and practiced _____ all week.When we
                                            ADVERB

met up the following week, we sounded much more _____.
                                                          ADJECTIVE

We decided to name ourselves the _____, and we practiced
                                      PLURAL NOUN

_____ times a week, even on the weekends. In a few months,
     NUMBER

we were really good, so we asked if we could play at the school dance. Mr.

_____, our principal, paid us _____ dollars. We
   SILLY WORD   NUMBER

were the _____ part of the whole dance!
              ADJECTIVE

MAD LIBS® is fun to play with friends, but you can also play it by yourself! To begin with, DO NOT look at the story on the page below. Fill in the blanks on this page with the words called for. Then, using the words you have selected, fill in the blank spaces in the story.

Now you've created your own hilarious MAD LIBS® game!

M.A.S.H.

ADJECTIVE _____

NUMBER _____

PLURAL NOUN _____

A PLACE _____

PERSON IN ROOM (MALE) _____

ADJECTIVE _____

A PLACE _____

ADJECTIVE _____

ADJECTIVE _____

NOUN _____

A PLACE _____

ADJECTIVE _____

NUMBER _____

NOUN _____

NUMBER _____

OCCUPATION _____

NOUN _____

ADJECTIVE _____

MAD LIBS®
M.A.S.H.

Congratulations! According to the M.A.S.H. (the ultimate sleepover game), your

future looks bright and _____. When you are _____ years
                              ADJECTIVE   NUMBER

old, you will meet the man of your _____ at (the) _____. His
                                      PLURAL NOUN   A PLACE

name will be _____. You will have a/an _____
              PERSON IN ROOM (MALE)   ADJECTIVE

wedding, and you will go to (the) _____ on your _____
                                    A PLACE   ADJECTIVE

honeymoon. When you return, you will move into a/an _____
                                                          ADJECTIVE

_____ in (the) _____. You will drive a/an
        NOUN   A PLACE

_____ car. Then, when you have been married for _____
    ADJECTIVE   NUMBER

years, you will have your first _____. You will go on to have
                                      NOUN

_____ more children. You will work as a/an _____
     NUMBER   OCCUPATION

until you retire and move to a tropical _____. Your M.A.S.H. future
                                            NOUN

looks prosperous and _____, so prepare to enjoy it!
                          ADJECTIVE

MAD LIBS® is fun to play with friends, but you can also play it by yourself! To begin with, DO NOT look at the story on the page below. Fill in the blanks on this page with the words called for. Then, using the words you have selected, fill in the blank spaces in the story.

Now you've created your own hilarious MAD LIBS® game!

WORLD SERIES BROADCAST

NOUN _____

PLURAL NOUN _____

NUMBER _____

NUMBER _____

NOUN _____

PART OF THE BODY (PLURAL) _____

PLURAL NOUN _____

ADJECTIVE _____

LAST NAME _____

VERB _____

NOUN _____

PERSON IN ROOM _____

NOUN _____

NOUN _____

NOUN _____

NOUN _____

NUMBER _____

ADJECTIVE _____

ADJECTIVE _____

MAD LIBS®
WORLD SERIES BROADCAST

Hard to believe—no, impossible to believe! Here we are in the bottom of the

ninth _____, the score is tied, there are two outs, and the
                NOUN

_____ are loaded . . . and yes, the count on the batter is
   PLURAL NOUN

_____ and _____. What an unbelievable moment! There
     NUMBER   NUMBER

isn't a fan sitting in his or her _____. They're all standing on their
                                         NOUN

_____, screaming at the top of their _____.
PART OF THE BODY (PLURAL)   PLURAL NOUN

Here comes the pitch. It's a ninety-mile-an-hour _____ ball. Foul!
                                                       ADJECTIVE

_____ just managed to _____ the ball with
   LAST NAME   VERB

the end of his _____. _____ rubs up another
                    NOUN   PERSON IN ROOM

_____, steps on the _____, and gets his/her
     NOUN   NOUN

_____ from the catcher squatting behind the _____.
   NOUN   NOUN

Here it comes . . . and there it goes! Ladies and gentlemen, it's a/an

_____-foot home run. Wow! What a/an _____ ending
   NUMBER   ADJECTIVE

to a truly _____ game.
               ADJECTIVE

MAD LIBS® is fun to play with friends, but you can also play it by yourself! To begin with, DO NOT look at the story on the page below. Fill in the blanks on this page with the words called for. Then, using the words you have selected, fill in the blank spaces in the story.

Now you've created your own hilarious MAD LIBS® game!

A REPORT CARD

PERSON IN ROOM (MALE) _____

A PLACE _____

ADVERB _____

PLURAL NOUN _____

VERB _____

VERB ENDING IN "ING" _____

ADJECTIVE _____

ADJECTIVE _____

ADJECTIVE _____

ADJECTIVE _____

PERSON IN ROOM (FEMALE) _____

NOUN _____

NOUN _____

ADVERB _____

PERSON IN ROOM _____

MAD LIBS®
A REPORT CARD

A report card for _____ *from* (the) _____.
PERSON IN ROOM (MALE)   A PLACE

Dear Parent:

Your child has been behaving _____. He refuses to cooperate with
ADVERB

his fellow _____ and likes to fidget and _____
PLURAL NOUN   VERB

in class when the teacher is _____. I am afraid I will have
VERB ENDING IN "ING"

to give him an Unsatisfactory in Deportment. His other grades are Spelling:

_____; Reading: _____; Science: _____;
ADJECTIVE   ADJECTIVE   ADJECTIVE

and Physical Education: _____. He had to be disciplined
ADJECTIVE

because he made faces at _____ last week. I do not think
PERSON IN ROOM (FEMALE)

your _____ is going to be an achiever. He seems more of a/an
NOUN

_____.
NOUN

Yours _____,
ADVERB

_____
PERSON IN ROOM

MAD LIBS® is fun to play with friends, but you can also play it by yourself! To begin with, DO NOT look at the story on the page below. Fill in the blanks on this page with the words called for. Then, using the words you have selected, fill in the blank spaces in the story.

Now you've created your own hilarious MAD LIBS® game!

SAGE ADVICE

VERB ENDING IN "ING" _____

PERSON IN ROOM _____

ADJECTIVE _____

ADJECTIVE _____

PLURAL NOUN _____

ADVERB _____

PLURAL NOUN _____

ADJECTIVE _____

PLURAL NOUN _____

NOUN _____

ADJECTIVE _____

PLURAL NOUN _____

PLURAL NOUN _____

VERB ENDING IN "ING" _____

NOUN _____

MAD LIBS®
SAGE ADVICE

According to the pioneer of downhill _____,
_____ VERB ENDING IN "ING"

_____,"When you ski, your _____ equipment
PERSON IN ROOM   ADJECTIVE

should be the equal of your _____ ability." Remember this
ADJECTIVE

sage advice when purchasing your first pair of _____. It is
PLURAL NOUN

_____ important to take many _____ into
ADVERB   PLURAL NOUN

consideration before plunking down _____ bucks for your
ADJECTIVE

_____. Your gender, your height, and your _____
PLURAL NOUN   NOUN

are all _____ factors in selecting a pair of _____
ADJECTIVE   PLURAL NOUN

that match your skills and _____. It goes without
PLURAL NOUN

_____: If you don't have the right skis, you're starting off on the
VERB ENDING IN "ING"

wrong _____.
NOUN

MAD LIBS® is fun to play with friends, but you can also play it by yourself! To begin with, DO NOT look at the story on the page below. Fill in the blanks on this page with the words called for. Then, using the words you have selected, fill in the blank spaces in the story.

Now you've created your own hilarious MAD LIBS® game!

MORE SAGE ADVICE

NOUN _____

NOUN _____

PLURAL NOUN _____

ADVERB _____

ADJECTIVE _____

PART OF THE BODY _____

NOUN _____

ADJECTIVE _____

NOUN _____

ADJECTIVE _____

NOUN _____

PART OF THE BODY _____

ADJECTIVE _____

NOUN _____

NOUN _____

ADJECTIVE _____

NOUN _____

NOUN _____

MAD LIBS®
MORE SAGE ADVICE

Beware! If your skiing equipment isn't top-of-the-_____, you put
NOUN

your _____ at risk. Here are some important _____
NOUN   PLURAL NOUN

to remember:

Ski Boots: Give careful thought to this important piece of equipment. Choose

_____. Together with ski bindings, these _____
ADVERB   ADJECTIVE

boots form the link between your skis and your _____.
PART OF THE BODY

Ski Bindings: As far as your safety is concerned, _____
NOUN

bindings are the most _____ pieces of _____ in
ADJECTIVE   NOUN

skiing. If you have any _____ questions, seek the help of a/an
ADJECTIVE

_____ professional.
NOUN

Ski Helmets: Protect your _____ by wearing a/an _____
PART OF THE BODY   ADJECTIVE

ski _____. Helmets absolutely help you avoid a serious
NOUN

_____ mishap.
NOUN

Ski Clothing: Get yourself some _____ underwear to keep your
ADJECTIVE

_____ warm. You also need a ski _____ to protect
NOUN   NOUN

your head and ears from frigid temperatures.

MAD LIBS® is fun to play with friends, but you can also play it by yourself! To begin with, DO NOT look at the story on the page below. Fill in the blanks on this page with the words called for. Then, using the words you have selected, fill in the blank spaces in the story.

Now you've created your own hilarious MAD LIBS® game!

PIRATES AND SEA MONSTERS

ADJECTIVE _____

ADJECTIVE _____

NOUN _____

NOUN _____

NOUN _____

VERB _____

SAME VERB _____

PLURAL NOUN _____

PLURAL NOUN _____

PLURAL NOUN _____

NOUN _____

PERSON IN ROOM _____

NOUN _____

PLURAL NOUN _____

NOUN _____

VERB (PAST TENSE) _____

PART OF THE BODY _____

NOUN _____

PART OF THE BODY _____

NOUN _____

ADJECTIVE _____

MAD LIBS®
PIRATES AND SEA MONSTERS

It was a/an _____ night, with fog so _____, you
        ADJECTIVE   ADJECTIVE

could barely see your _____ in front of your _____.
                         NOUN   NOUN

The only sound was the groan of the tired _____ and the soft
                                       NOUN

wind, which seemed to whisper, "_____ . . . _____ . . ."
                               VERB   SAME VERB

Suddenly, _____ shot out of the ocean like _____
          PLURAL NOUN   PLURAL NOUN

on the Fourth of July. *Bang! Pow!* They grabbed for _____
                                            PLURAL NOUN

to bring down to the bottom of the sea—to Davy Jones's locker. The dreaded

_____ monster, _____, was as big as a giant
       NOUN   PERSON IN ROOM

_____ and it smelled like rotting _____. I hid
       NOUN   PLURAL NOUN

inside a/an _____ and _____ as the monster
            NOUN   VERB (PAST TENSE)

sucked the _____ right off one of my shipmates! I was scared
          PART OF THE BODY

out of my _____, and my _____ almost stopped
            NOUN   PART OF THE BODY

beating! But, lucky for you, I escaped with my _____ and lived to
                                       NOUN

tell the _____ tale!
       ADJECTIVE

MAD LIBS® is fun to play with friends, but you can also play it by yourself! To begin with, DO NOT look at the story on the page below. Fill in the blanks on this page with the words called for. Then, using the words you have selected, fill in the blank spaces in the story.

Now you've created your own hilarious MAD LIBS® game!

EAT, DRINK, AND BE SICK

NOUN _____

ADJECTIVE _____

ADJECTIVE _____

NOUN _____

NOUN _____

PLURAL NOUN _____

PLURAL NOUN _____

NOUN _____

PART OF THE BODY _____

PLURAL NOUN _____

ADVERB _____

PLURAL NOUN _____

PLURAL NOUN _____

PLURAL NOUN _____

LETTER OF THE ALPHABET _____

MAD LIBS®

EAT, DRINK, AND BE SICK

An inspector from the Department of Health and _____
<u>NOUN</u>

Services paid a surprise visit to our _____ school cafeteria.
<u>ADJECTIVE</u>

The lunch special, prepared by our _____ dietician, was
<u>ADJECTIVE</u>

spaghetti and _____-balls with a choice of either a/an
<u>NOUN</u>

_____ salad or french _____. The inspector
<u>NOUN</u> <u>PLURAL NOUN</u>

found the meat-_____ to be overcooked and discovered a live
<u>PLURAL NOUN</u>

_____ in the fries, causing him to have a/an _____
<u>NOUN</u> <u>PART OF THE BODY</u>

ache. In response, he threw up all over his _____. In his report,
<u>PLURAL NOUN</u>

the inspector _____ recommended that the school cafeteria serve
<u>ADVERB</u>

only nutritious _____ as well as low-calorie _____,
<u>PLURAL NOUN</u> <u>PLURAL NOUN</u>

and that all of the saturated _____ be eliminated. He rated the
<u>PLURAL NOUN</u>

cafeteria a/an _____-minus.
<u>LETTER OF THE ALPHABET</u>

MAD LIBS® is fun to play with friends, but you can also play it by yourself! To begin with, DO NOT look at the story on the page below. Fill in the blanks on this page with the words called for. Then, using the words you have selected, fill in the blank spaces in the story.

Now you've created your own hilarious MAD LIBS® game!

REPORT BY STUDENT PROTEST COMMITTEE

A PLACE _____

ADJECTIVE _____

PLURAL NOUN _____

PERSON IN ROOM (MALE) _____

PART OF THE BODY _____

ARTICLE OF CLOTHING _____

PLURAL NOUN _____

NOUN _____

NOUN _____

ADJECTIVE _____

ADJECTIVE _____

PLURAL NOUN _____

MAD LIBS®
REPORT BY STUDENT PROTEST COMMITTEE

Fellow Students of (the) _____! We the members of the Students
                                A PLACE

for a/an _____ Society are meeting here to decide what action
           ADJECTIVE

to take about the Dean of _____. He has just fired our friend,
                           PLURAL NOUN

Professor _____, because he wore his _____
         PERSON IN ROOM (MALE)   PART OF THE BODY

long, and because he dressed in a/an _____ and wore
                                ARTICLE OF CLOTHING

old _____. Next week, we are going to protest by taking
     PLURAL NOUN

over the _____ building and kidnapping the Assistant
               NOUN

_____. We also will demand that all students have the right to
   NOUN

wear _____ hair and _____ beards. Remember
      ADJECTIVE   ADJECTIVE

our slogan: "Down with _____."
                  PLURAL NOUN

MAD LIBS® is fun to play with friends, but you can also play it by yourself! To begin with, DO NOT look at the story on the page below. Fill in the blanks on this page with the words called for. Then, using the words you have selected, fill in the blank spaces in the story.

Now you've created your own hilarious MAD LIBS® game!

FAMOUS QUOTES FROM THE AMERICAN REVOLUTION

NOUN _____

NOUN _____

COLOR _____

PART OF THE BODY (PLURAL) _____

NOUN _____

PLURAL NOUN _____

VERB ENDING IN "ING" _____

NOUN _____

PLURAL NOUN _____

PLURAL NOUN _____

ADJECTIVE _____

NOUN _____

MAD LIBS

FAMOUS QUOTES FROM THE AMERICAN REVOLUTION

Nathan Hale said: "I regret that I have but one _____ to give for
                                                        NOUN

my _____."
        NOUN

William Prescott said: "Don't fire until you see the _____ of their
                                                                COLOR

_____."
PART OF THE BODY (PLURAL)

Patrick Henry said: "Give me liberty or give me _____."
                                                            NOUN

Paul Revere said: "The _____ are _____."
                            PLURAL NOUN   VERB ENDING IN "ING"

John Hancock said: "I wrote my _____ large so the king could
                                        NOUN

read it without his _____."
                        PLURAL NOUN

Thomas Jefferson said: "All _____ are created equal . . . They are
                                    PLURAL NOUN

endowed by their creator with certain _____ rights; that among
                                                ADJECTIVE

these are life, liberty, and the pursuit of _____."
                                                    NOUN

MAD LIBS® is fun to play with friends, but you can also play it by yourself! To begin with, DO NOT look at the story on the page below. Fill in the blanks on this page with the words called for. Then, using the words you have selected, fill in the blank spaces in the story.

Now you've created your own hilarious MAD LIBS® game!

A FAMILY CAR TRIP

PART OF THE BODY _____

NOUN _____

NOUN _____

NOUN _____

PLURAL NOUN _____

PLURAL NOUN _____

ADJECTIVE _____

PLURAL NOUN _____

NOUN _____

PLURAL NOUN _____

EXCLAMATION _____

NOUN _____

ADJECTIVE _____

PLURAL NOUN _____

TYPE OF LIQUID _____

NOUN _____

ADJECTIVE _____

MAD LIBS®
A FAMILY CAR TRIP

To be performed by three volunteers.

KID: I'm starved, Mom. My _____ is growling.
PART OF THE BODY

MOM: I think you've had enough _____ food today. You ate
NOUN

enough to choke a/an _____.
NOUN

KID: But I'm a growing _____. Dad, can we stop and get a
NOUN

hamburger with _____ and _____?
PLURAL NOUN   PLURAL NOUN

DAD: You just had a/an _____ breakfast!
ADJECTIVE

KID: No, I didn't. All I had was a couple of scrambled _____.
PLURAL NOUN

MOM: How about those five pieces of buttered _____, plus that
NOUN

stack of _____?
PLURAL NOUN

KID: _____! I have to go to the _____-room. Can
EXCLAMATION   NOUN

we stop? I have to go real _____!
ADJECTIVE

DAD: Okay. It'll give me a chance to stretch my _____.
PLURAL NOUN

MOM: Stop at that diner. I can use a cup of strong _____.
TYPE OF LIQUID

KID: As long as we're stopping, can I have a grilled _____ and
NOUN

some _____ fries? That will hold me until lunch.
ADJECTIVE

MAD LIBS® is fun to play with friends, but you can also play it by yourself! To begin with, DO NOT look at the story on the page below. Fill in the blanks on this page with the words called for. Then, using the words you have selected, fill in the blank spaces in the story.

Now you've created your own hilarious MAD LIBS® game!

REVIEW OF
A DINOSAUR MOVIE

VERB ENDING IN "ING" _____

ADJECTIVE _____

ADJECTIVE _____

ADJECTIVE _____

ADJECTIVE _____

NOUN _____

PERSON IN ROOM _____

ADJECTIVE _____

NOUN _____

ADJECTIVE _____

PLURAL NOUN _____

PART OF THE BODY (PLURAL) _____

NOUN _____

PLURAL NOUN _____

LETTER OF THE ALPHABET _____

NOUN _____

MAD LIBS®
REVIEW OF A DINOSAUR MOVIE

Despite its title, *Dinosaurs Are for* _____ is far from being
VERB ENDING IN "ING"

a/an _____ comedy. It is really a/an _____ horror
ADJECTIVE   ADJECTIVE

movie. From its _____ opening until its _____
ADJECTIVE   ADJECTIVE

ending, it keeps you sitting on the edge of your _____. In this
NOUN

film, the ever-popular _____ gives the performance of
PERSON IN ROOM

his/her _____ career. He/She plays the role of a scientist who, in
ADJECTIVE

searching for the Fountain of _____, accidentally discovers a/an
NOUN

_____ beast that feasts on living _____. The last ten
ADJECTIVE   PLURAL NOUN

minutes of the movie are scary enough to make your _____
PART OF THE BODY (PLURAL)

pop out of your _____ and your _____ stand on
NOUN   PLURAL NOUN

end. The movie is rated _____, meaning children under twelve
LETTER OF THE ALPHABET

must be accompanied by a/an _____.
NOUN

MAD LIBS® is fun to play with friends, but you can also play it by yourself! To begin with, DO NOT look at the story on the page below. Fill in the blanks on this page with the words called for. Then, using the words you have selected, fill in the blank spaces in the story.

Now you've created your own hilarious MAD LIBS® game!

THE KING OF CREEPY

FIRST NAME (MALE) _____

ADJECTIVE _____

ADJECTIVE _____

TYPE OF FOOD _____

ANIMAL _____

PLURAL NOUN _____

A PLACE _____

VERB ENDING IN "ING" _____

LAST NAME _____

LAST NAME _____

ADJECTIVE _____

NUMBER _____

PLURAL NOUN _____

ADJECTIVE _____

ADJECTIVE _____

NOUN _____

TYPE OF LIQUID _____

ADVERB _____

MAD LIBS®
THE KING OF CREEPY

_____ King has written some really _____, spooky
   FIRST NAME (MALE)   ADJECTIVE

books that have been made into super-_____ movies. For instance,
                                   ADJECTIVE

there was _Children of the_ _____ and _Cujo the_ _____.
                           TYPE OF FOOD   ANIMAL

And then there was another one about _____, which was
                                    PLURAL NOUN

called _Pet_ (the) _____." A very successful movie was _The_
                  A PLACE

_____, which starred Jack _____ and Shelly
  VERB ENDING IN "ING"   LAST NAME

_____. It was Jack's first big movie and since then he has become
  LAST NAME

a/an _____ star and has been nominated for _____
     ADJECTIVE   NUMBER

Academy _____. There are other very _____ scary
        PLURAL NOUN   ADJECTIVE

films that Mr. King did not write. For instance, the _____ classic
                                      ADJECTIVE

called _The Chain Saw_ _____, which can really curdle a person's
                        NOUN

_____. If you see any of these movies, chances are you won't
  TYPE OF LIQUID

sleep very _____ that night.
         ADVERB

MAD LIBS® is fun to play with friends, but you can also play it by yourself! To begin with, DO NOT look at the story on the page below. Fill in the blanks on this page with the words called for. Then, using the words you have selected, fill in the blank spaces in the story.

Now you've created your own hilarious MAD LIBS® game!

CELL PHONES

NOUN _____

PART OF THE BODY _____

PLURAL NOUN _____

NOUN _____

PLURAL NOUN _____

PLURAL NOUN _____

PLURAL NOUN _____

PLURAL NOUN _____

VERB ENDING IN "ING" _____

ADVERB _____

PART OF THE BODY _____

VERB _____

ADJECTIVE _____

NOUN _____

PLURAL NOUN _____

NOUN _____

NOUN _____

MAD LIBS®
CELL PHONES

No matter where you are these days, you're bound to run into someone with

a cellular _____ attached to his/her _____. Even
             NOUN   PART OF THE BODY

young _____ have _____ phones. Unfortunately,
         PLURAL NOUN   NOUN

they seem to bring out the worst _____ in people. Most cell-
                              PLURAL NOUN

phone users talk with raised _____ in restaurants, museums,
                        PLURAL NOUN

_____, and even in women's and men's _____.
  PLURAL NOUN   PLURAL NOUN

Cell-phone users think nothing of talking at the same time they are

_____ their cars. This can be _____ dangerous,
VERB ENDING IN "ING"   ADVERB

especially when they take their _____ off the road as they
                        PART OF THE BODY

_____. Pedestrian phoners are also a/an _____
    VERB   ADJECTIVE

hazard. Preoccupied with their conversations, they can easily ignore a red

_____ and step in front of oncoming _____,
   NOUN   PLURAL NOUN

causing all kinds of _____ accidents and _____ pileups.
           NOUN   NOUN

MAD LIBS® is fun to play with friends, but you can also play it by yourself! To begin with, DO NOT look at the story on the page below. Fill in the blanks on this page with the words called for. Then, using the words you have selected, fill in the blank spaces in the story.

Now you've created your own hilarious MAD LIBS® game!

PROPER CARE OF THE SCALP

ADJECTIVE _____

ADJECTIVE _____

ADJECTIVE _____

ADJECTIVE _____

NOUN _____

PLURAL NOUN _____

ADVERB _____

ADJECTIVE _____

NOUN _____

NOUN _____

NOUN _____

ADJECTIVE _____

NOUN _____

NOUN _____

MAD LIBS®
PROPER CARE OF THE SCALP

Don't neglect your scalp! Even though you don't know it, your scalp may be

_____. This can cause your hair to turn _____ and
  ADJECTIVE   ADJECTIVE

_____. A/An _____ scalp is due to overactivity on
  ADJECTIVE   ADJECTIVE

the part of the _____ gland and to excessive production of the
                 NOUN

_____ normally present in the skin. For a healthy scalp, wash your
  PLURAL NOUN

head _____ every night in _____ water and then take a
      ADVERB   ADJECTIVE

hot _____ shampoo. Then massage your _____ for five
    NOUN   NOUN

minutes with a sharp _____. If you suffer from _____
                  NOUN   ADJECTIVE

hair, soak your _____ regularly in a/an _____ of
           NOUN   NOUN

vinegar. Good luck!

MAD LIBS® is fun to play with friends, but you can also play it by yourself! To begin with, DO NOT look at the story on the page below. Fill in the blanks on this page with the words called for. Then, using the words you have selected, fill in the blank spaces in the story.

Now you've created your own hilarious MAD LIBS® game!

OUR SOLAR SYSTEM

ADJECTIVE _____

NOUN _____

ADJECTIVE _____

PLURAL NOUN _____

ADVERB _____

VERB ENDING IN "ING" _____

PLURAL NOUN _____

ADJECTIVE _____

PLURAL NOUN _____

FIRST NAME _____

ADJECTIVE _____

NUMBER _____

FIRST NAME _____

FIRST NAME _____

FIRST NAME _____

FIRST NAME _____

FIRST NAME _____

FIRST NAME _____

PLURAL NOUN _____

MAD LIBS®

OUR SOLAR SYSTEM

When we look up into the sky on a/an ____________ summer night, we
ADJECTIVE
see millions of tiny spots of light. Each one represents a/an ____________
NOUN
which is the center of a/an ____________ solar system with dozens of
ADJECTIVE
____________ revolving ____________ around a distant sun.
PLURAL NOUN ADVERB
Sometimes these suns expand and begin ____________ their neighbors.
VERB ENDING IN "ING"
Soon they will become so big, they will turn into ____________.
PLURAL NOUN
Eventually they subside and become ____________ giants or perhaps
ADJECTIVE
black ____________. Our own planet, which we call ____________,
PLURAL NOUN FIRST NAME
circles around our ____________ sun ____________
ADJECTIVE NUMBER
of times every year. There are eight other planets in our solar system. They are
named ____________, ____________, ____________,
FIRST NAME FIRST NAME FIRST NAME
____________, ____________, ____________, Jupiter, and
FIRST NAME FIRST NAME FIRST NAME
Mars. Scientists who study these planets are called ____________.
PLURAL NOUN

MAD LIBS® is fun to play with friends, but you can also play it by yourself! To begin with, DO NOT look at the story on the page below. Fill in the blanks on this page with the words called for. Then, using the words you have selected, fill in the blank spaces in the story.

Now you've created your own hilarious MAD LIBS® game!

EXPLORERS

PERSON IN ROOM _____

CELEBRITY _____

NOUN _____

PLURAL NOUN _____

NOUN _____

ADJECTIVE _____

NOUN _____

A PLACE _____

NUMBER _____

ADJECTIVE _____

TYPE OF LIQUID _____

ADJECTIVE _____

ADJECTIVE _____

VERB ENDING IN "ING" _____

PLURAL NOUN _____

NOUN _____

ADJECTIVE _____

PLURAL NOUN _____

MAD LIBS®
EXPLORERS

Camping is a good way to learn to be an explorer. Famous explorers have

been Columbus, Pizarro, Balboa, and _____, who discovered
                                         PERSON IN ROOM

_____. Hernando Cortes was a Spanish _____
      CELEBRITY   NOUN

who came to South America and conquered the _____.
                                                PLURAL NOUN

Francisco Pizarro was another famous _____. He was the first
                                          NOUN

man to see the _____ Pacific _____. Ponce de
                    ADJECTIVE   NOUN

Leon discovered Puerto Rico, Florida, and (the) _____
                                                    A PLACE

in 1512. He spent _____ years in Florida trying to find a/an
                       NUMBER

_____ fountain of youth. He believed that _____
      ADJECTIVE   TYPE OF LIQUID

from this fountain would make him eternally _____. He marched
                                                 ADJECTIVE

his _____ troops through swamps _____ with
        ADJECTIVE   VERB ENDING IN "ING"

alligators and _____ in search of this miracle _____
                    PLURAL NOUN   NOUN

but never found anything that would make him _____. The only
                                                  ADJECTIVE

thing he found were thousands of _____ from the north
                                      PLURAL NOUN

who had come there for a vacation.

MAD LIBS® is fun to play with friends, but you can also play it by yourself! To begin with, DO NOT look at the story on the page below. Fill in the blanks on this page with the words called for. Then, using the words you have selected, fill in the blank spaces in the story.

Now you've created your own hilarious MAD LIBS® game!

A VEGETABLE GARDEN

PLURAL NOUN _____

ADJECTIVE _____

PLURAL NOUN _____

PLURAL NOUN _____

PLURAL NOUN _____

NOUN _____

PLURAL NOUN _____

NOUN _____

ADJECTIVE _____

PLURAL NOUN _____

PLURAL NOUN _____

PLURAL NOUN _____

ADJECTIVE _____

NOUN _____

ADJECTIVE _____

MAD LIBS®
A VEGETABLE GARDEN

Planting a vegetable garden is not only fun, it also helps save _____.

PLURAL NOUN

You will need a piece of _____ land at least twenty feet long

ADJECTIVE

and twenty-five _____ wide. You may need a fence to keep the

PLURAL NOUN

_____ and _____ out. As soon as the cold

PLURAL NOUN   PLURAL NOUN

weather is over, you can get out there with your _____ and

NOUN

plant all kinds of _____. Then in a few months, you will have

PLURAL NOUN

homegrown corn on the _____, lovely, _____

NOUN   ADJECTIVE

tomatoes with fresh green _____ and, best of all, vine-ripened

PLURAL NOUN

_____. Homegrown _____ are much more

PLURAL NOUN   PLURAL NOUN

nutritious than _____ vegetables because they contain natural

ADJECTIVE

_____ and _____ vitamins.

NOUN   ADJECTIVE

MAD LIBS® is fun to play with friends, but you can also play it by yourself! To begin with, DO NOT look at the story on the page below. Fill in the blanks on this page with the words called for. Then, using the words you have selected, fill in the blank spaces in the story.

Now you've created your own hilarious MAD LIBS® game!

PIRATE LOYALTY OATH (ARTICLES OF AGREEMENT)

COLOR _____

NOUN _____

PART OF THE BODY _____

TYPE OF LIQUID _____

PART OF THE BODY _____

ADJECTIVE _____

NOUN _____

PLURAL NOUN _____

NUMBER _____

PLURAL NOUN _____

NOUN _____

ADJECTIVE _____

NOUN _____

NOUN _____

ADJECTIVE _____

VERB _____

NOUN _____

PLURAL NOUN _____

MAD LIBS®

PIRATE LOYALTY OATH (ARTICLES OF AGREEMENT)

Many a boy and girl dream of sailing the ocean _____ aboard a/an
                                                        COLOR

_____ ship. But that dream becomes a nightmare when they learn
        NOUN

that they have to prick their _____ and sign an oath of loyalty
                                PART OF THE BODY

with their own _____ before they can set _____
                  TYPE OF LIQUID   PART OF THE BODY

aboard the ship. This is how one _____ oath might have read:
                                      ADJECTIVE

"Any buccaneer who disobeys the captain's orders will be put under lock and

_____ and fed only bread and _____ for
        NOUN   PLURAL NOUN

_____ days and _____. Any shipmate who strikes
      NUMBER   PLURAL NOUN

a fellow crew-_____ shall be tied to a/an _____
                    NOUN   ADJECTIVE

sail from sunup to _____-down. Any _____ who
                          NOUN   NOUN

does not keep his or her sword _____ and musket ready to
                                      ADJECTIVE

_____ will be thrown over the _____ and fed to
        VERB   NOUN

the _____."
      PLURAL NOUN

MAD LIBS® is fun to play with friends, but you can also play it by yourself! To begin with, DO NOT look at the story on the page below. Fill in the blanks on this page with the words called for. Then, using the words you have selected, fill in the blank spaces in the story.

Now you've created your own hilarious MAD LIBS® game!

ODE TO A CUPCAKE

ADJECTIVE _____

NOUN _____

ADJECTIVE _____

PART OF THE BODY _____

NOUN _____

NOUN _____

ADJECTIVE _____

NOUN _____

NOUN _____

VERB _____

ADJECTIVE _____

ADJECTIVE _____

PLURAL NOUN _____

PART OF THE BODY _____

NOUN _____

ADJECTIVE _____

TYPE OF LIQUID _____

ADVERB _____

MAD LIBS®
ODE TO A CUPCAKE

O, _____ cupcake, how I love thee! Let me count the ways.
    ADJECTIVE

Your frosting is as sweet as a summer's _____. Just the
    NOUN

_____ thought of you makes my _____ water.
ADJECTIVE   PART OF THE BODY

Whether you are made of vanilla _____ topped with chocolate
    NOUN

butter-_____ frosting or made of _____ cake with
    NOUN   ADJECTIVE

_____-flavored frosting, it does not make a/an _____
    NOUN   NOUN

of difference to me. I love you no matter how you _____. And, O!
    VERB

There are so many _____ ways to devour your _____
    ADJECTIVE   ADJECTIVE

deliciousness. One may lick all the _____ off the top first—or
    PLURAL NOUN

simply shove you into one's _____ in a single _____.
    PART OF THE BODY   NOUN

All a person needs is a/an _____ glass of cool _____,
    ADJECTIVE   TYPE OF LIQUID

and the cupcake experience is _____ complete!
    ADVERB

MAD LIBS® is fun to play with friends, but you can also play it by yourself! To begin with, DO NOT look at the story on the page below. Fill in the blanks on this page with the words called for. Then, using the words you have selected, fill in the blank spaces in the story.

Now you've created your own hilarious MAD LIBS® game!

THE FARMER

PLURAL NOUN _____

NOUN _____

PLURAL NOUN _____

ADJECTIVE _____

PLURAL NOUN _____

ADJECTIVE _____

TYPE OF LIQUID _____

PLURAL NOUN _____

NOUN _____

PLURAL NOUN _____

ADJECTIVE _____

MAD LIBS®
THE FARMER

Farmers work very hard planting wheat and _____. They begin
PLURAL NOUN

by plowing their _____, and if they don't have a tractor, they use
NOUN

_____. Then they plant _____ seeds, and by the
PLURAL NOUN   ADJECTIVE

next fall, they have many acres of _____. Tomatoes are harder to
PLURAL NOUN

raise. They grow on _____ bushes and the farmer sprays them
ADJECTIVE

with _____ to keep the bugs off. The easiest things to grow
TYPE OF LIQUID

are green _____, but the farmer must be very careful to make
PLURAL NOUN

sure worms don't get into his _____. Farmers also raise onions,
NOUN

cabbages, lettuce, and _____. But no matter what they grow,
PLURAL NOUN

farmers really lead a/an _____ life.
ADJECTIVE

MAD LIBS® is fun to play with friends, but you can also play it by yourself! To begin with, DO NOT look at the story on the page below. Fill in the blanks on this page with the words called for. Then, using the words you have selected, fill in the blank spaces in the story.

Now you've created your own hilarious MAD LIBS® game!

ASTROLOGY AND ASTRONOMY

ADJECTIVE _____

PLURAL NOUN _____

PLURAL NOUN _____

NOUN _____

NOUN _____

NOUN _____

PLURAL NOUN _____

PLURAL NOUN _____

NOUN _____

PLURAL NOUN _____

NOUN _____

NOUN _____

NOUN _____

NOUN _____

MAD LIBS®
ASTROLOGY AND ASTRONOMY

People often confuse astrology with astronomy. Astrology is the _____
ADJECTIVE

study of the influence of the position of the moon and _____
PLURAL NOUN

on human _____. Your daily horoscope gives you advice such as
PLURAL NOUN

whether or not you should get out of _____ in the morning and
NOUN

go to work, marry the _____ of your dreams, or invest money in
NOUN

the stock _____. Astronomy is a study by _____ of
NOUN   PLURAL NOUN

heavenly _____. These scientists conduct studies of the heavens
PLURAL NOUN

by looking through a/an _____ and tracking the movements of
NOUN

stars and _____ across the sky. It was astronomy that informed
PLURAL NOUN

us about such constellations as the Big _____, the Little
NOUN

_____, and the Milky _____. Without astronomy,
NOUN   NOUN

we would never have been able to send a person to the _____.
NOUN

MAD LIBS® is fun to play with friends, but you can also play it by yourself! To begin with, DO NOT look at the story on the page below. Fill in the blanks on this page with the words called for. Then, using the words you have selected, fill in the blank spaces in the story.

Now you've created your own hilarious MAD LIBS® game!

MOST LIKELY TO . . .

NUMBER _____

VERB _____

PERSON IN ROOM (FEMALE) _____

VERB _____

A PLACE _____

NOUN _____

SILLY WORD _____

ADJECTIVE _____

VERB _____

PERSON IN ROOM (FEMALE) _____

A PLACE _____

NUMBER _____

NOUN _____

SILLY WORD _____

OCCUPATION _____

VERB _____

VERB _____

ADJECTIVE _____

A PLACE _____

VERB ENDING IN "ING" _____

PLURAL NOUN _____

MAD LIBS®
MOST LIKELY TO . . .

_____ pages of our yearbook were dedicated to "The

NUMBER

Person Most Likely To . . ." when we _____ up. My best friend,

VERB

_____, was voted most likely to _____ in (the)

PERSON IN ROOM (FEMALE)   VERB

_____, because she wants to be a movie _____ when

A PLACE   NOUN

she grows up. Peter _____ was voted most _____,

SILLY WORD   ADJECTIVE

because all the girls in my class _____ when he walks by.

VERB

_____ was voted most likely to graduate from (the)

PERSON IN ROOM (FEMALE)

_____ with honors, because she got a/an _____

A PLACE   NUMBER

on every _____ test last semester. My friend _____

NOUN   SILLY WORD

got everyone's vote for the girl most likely to be a/an _____,

OCCUPATION

because she loves to make people _____. And me? I was named

VERB

the most likely to _____, because of all my _____

VERB   ADJECTIVE

adventures traveling to (the) _____ and _____

A PLACE   VERB ENDING IN "ING"

through the Rocky _____.

PLURAL NOUN

MAD LIBS® is fun to play with friends, but you can also play it by yourself! To begin with, DO NOT look at the story on the page below. Fill in the blanks on this page with the words called for. Then, using the words you have selected, fill in the blank spaces in the story.

Now you've created your own hilarious MAD LIBS® game!

REVIEWS OF ENTERTAINERS APPEARING AT RESORTS

FIRST NAME (MALE) _____

FIRST NAME (FEMALE) _____

ADJECTIVE _____

NOUN _____

PLURAL NOUN _____

ADJECTIVE _____

PERSON IN ROOM (MALE) _____

SILLY WORD _____

PLURAL NOUN _____

ADJECTIVE _____

ARTICLE OF CLOTHING _____

VERB (PAST TENSE) _____

PERSON IN ROOM _____

PERSON IN ROOM _____

PERSON IN ROOM _____

ADJECTIVE _____

NOUN _____

NUMBER _____

CELEBRITY _____

MAD LIBS®
REVIEWS OF ENTERTAINERS APPEARING AT RESORTS

- _____ and _____ made their debit as a/an
  FIRST NAME (MALE)   FIRST NAME (FEMALE)

  _____ singing act at the _____ Lounge. The
  ADJECTIVE   NOUN

  songs they sang ranged from a series of crowd-pleasing old _____
                                                                PLURAL NOUN

  to _____ songs.
     ADJECTIVE

- A young comedian named _____ opened at the
                          PERSON IN ROOM (MALE)

  _____ Hotel last night. He began with a monologue of one-
  SILLY WORD

  line _____, which garnered _____ laughter
       PLURAL NOUN   ADJECTIVE

  from the audience. Then he donned a comical _____ and
                                               ARTICLE OF CLOTHING

  _____.
  VERB (PAST TENSE)

- _____ and _____, the dancing twins, headline
  PERSON IN ROOM   PERSON IN ROOM

  the _____ Hotel with their _____ act. The twins
      PERSON IN ROOM   ADJECTIVE

  present their version of the _____. For the grand finale, the duo
                                NOUN

  does a _____-step to the music of _____.
         NUMBER   CELEBRITY

MAD LIBS® is fun to play with friends, but you can also play it by yourself! To begin with, DO NOT look at the story on the page below. Fill in the blanks on this page with the words called for. Then, using the words you have selected, fill in the blank spaces in the story.

Now you've created your own hilarious MAD LIBS® game!

DOUBLE FAULT

ADJECTIVE _____

PART OF THE BODY _____

PLURAL NOUN _____

PERSON IN ROOM (FEMALE) _____

PERSON IN ROOM (FEMALE) _____

NOUN _____

NOUN _____

PLURAL NOUN _____

PART OF THE BODY _____

NUMBER _____

PART OF THE BODY (PLURAL) _____

PLURAL NOUN _____

NOUN _____

NUMBER _____

ADJECTIVE _____

ADJECTIVE _____

VERB ENDING IN "ING" _____

PART OF THE BODY _____

MAD LIBS®
DOUBLE FAULT

It's embarrassing that in a family of _____ athletes, I'm the only
                                        ADJECTIVE

one without any hand-_____ coordination. So I asked my two
                      PART OF THE BODY

_____, _____ and _____,
PLURAL NOUN   PERSON IN ROOM (FEMALE)   PERSON IN ROOM (FEMALE)

for help. They're both on the varsity _____ team. I didn't have
                                       NOUN

the slightest _____ of what I was getting into. My two sweet
              NOUN

_____ became unbelievable trainers. They had me doing daily
PLURAL NOUN

push-ups, sit-ups, and deep _____ bends, and I was running
                            PART OF THE BODY

_____ miles a day to strengthen my _____.
NUMBER   PART OF THE BODY (PLURAL)

I also had to do a series of deep-breathing _____ designed to
                                            PLURAL NOUN

improve my _____ capacity. It was a grueling _____
           NOUN   NUMBER

months before my _____ sisters deemed me ready for the
                 ADJECTIVE

_____ moment. Unfortunately, it never happened. As I was
ADJECTIVE

_____ at tryouts, I tripped and broke my _____.
VERB ENDING IN "ING"   PART OF THE BODY

Anyone up for chess?

MAD LIBS® is fun to play with friends, but you can also play it by yourself! To begin with, DO NOT look at the story on the page below. Fill in the blanks on this page with the words called for. Then, using the words you have selected, fill in the blank spaces in the story.

Now you've created your own hilarious MAD LIBS® game!

THE ENVIRONMENT

PLURAL NOUN _____

VERB ENDING IN "ING" _____

VERB ENDING IN "ING" _____

NUMBER _____

NOUN _____

PLURAL NOUN _____

NOUN _____

PLURAL NOUN _____

PLURAL NOUN _____

A PLACE _____

TYPE OF LIQUID _____

ADJECTIVE _____

ADJECTIVE _____

PLURAL NOUN _____

PLURAL NOUN _____

ADJECTIVE _____

ADJECTIVE _____

MAD LIBS®
THE ENVIRONMENT

Today, many scientists and college _____ tell us that we are
                                          PLURAL NOUN

_____ the atmosphere and _____ the water
  VERB ENDING IN "ING"   VERB ENDING IN "ING"

all over the world. In fact, in about _____ years, the air will be
                                              NUMBER

eighty percent _____ because we are cutting down all of the
                      NOUN

_____ in the Brazilian _____ forest. Here in the
  PLURAL NOUN   NOUN

United States, many manufacturers of toxic things like _____
                                                              PLURAL NOUN

or _____ take their waste material and dump it into the ocean
      PLURAL NOUN

or in (the) _____. We often have to close beaches and keep
                 A PLACE

people from going into the _____ because it is so polluted.
                                 TYPE OF LIQUID

But there are some _____ things you can do to help protect our
                          ADJECTIVE

environment. You can write _____ letters to your congressperson.
                                 ADJECTIVE

You can also recycle _____. With just a bit of effort, all
                            PLURAL NOUN

_____ can help to make our planet _____ and
  PLURAL NOUN   ADJECTIVE

_____ again.
  ADJECTIVE

MAD LIBS® is fun to play with friends, but you can also play it by yourself! To begin with, DO NOT look at the story on the page below. Fill in the blanks on this page with the words called for. Then, using the words you have selected, fill in the blank spaces in the story.

Now you've created your own hilarious MAD LIBS® game!

THINGS TO DO THIS WEEKEND

LAST NAME _____

ADJECTIVE _____

PLURAL NOUN _____

PLURAL NOUN _____

NOUN _____

ADJECTIVE _____

NOUN _____

ADVERB _____

NOUN _____

ADJECTIVE _____

PLURAL NOUN _____

PERSON IN ROOM _____

ADJECTIVE _____

NOUN _____

ADJECTIVE _____

ADJECTIVE _____

NOUN _____

NOUN _____

ADJECTIVE _____

MAD LIBS®
THINGS TO DO THIS WEEKEND

FILM

_____ Theaters offers a/an _____
       LAST NAME   ADJECTIVE

program of foreign _____ never before seen in American
                          PLURAL NOUN

_____. The first film to be shown will be *Henry and the*
     PLURAL NOUN

_____. This is the _____ love story of a man and
     NOUN   ADJECTIVE

his _____. It will be shown _____ until the end
        NOUN   ADVERB

of the _____.
         NOUN

STAGE

Appearing in our _____ theater for the next three _____
                    ADJECTIVE   PLURAL NOUN

is _____, that very _____ star of stage, screen, and
    PERSON IN ROOM   ADJECTIVE

_____. He/She will be appearing with our _____
     NOUN   ADJECTIVE

repertory company in nightly performances of William Shakespeare's

_____ comedy, *A Midsummer Night's* _____.
   ADJECTIVE   NOUN

Tickets can be purchased now at the _____ office by telephone,
                                       NOUN

fax, or _____ card.
           ADJECTIVE

MAD LIBS® is fun to play with friends, but you can also play it by yourself! To begin with, DO NOT look at the story on the page below. Fill in the blanks on this page with the words called for. Then, using the words you have selected, fill in the blank spaces in the story.

Now you've created your own hilarious MAD LIBS® game!

MUSIC

NOUN _____

NOUN _____

ADJECTIVE _____

ADJECTIVE _____

PART OF THE BODY (PLURAL) _____

PART OF THE BODY (PLURAL) _____

ADJECTIVE _____

NOUN _____

NOUN _____

NOUN _____

PLURAL NOUN _____

ADJECTIVE _____

PLURAL NOUN _____

NOUN _____

MAD LIBS®
MUSIC

"Music is the soul of the _____," said Pluto. "Music is music
                              NOUN

is music," said rap _____ I.B. Cool. These two _____
                     NOUN   ADJECTIVE

philosophers were right on! When the beat is right, who among us hasn't felt

the _____ urge to snap his/her _____
        ADJECTIVE   PART OF THE BODY (PLURAL)

or stomp his/her _____ or break out in a/an
                 PART OF THE BODY (PLURAL)

_____ _____? There's no denying that music,
     ADJECTIVE   NOUN

whether it's a classical _____ by Beethoven or a contemporary
                             NOUN

_____ by the Backstreet _____, is a/an
     NOUN   PLURAL NOUN

_____ influence on our daily _____. Music does
   ADJECTIVE   PLURAL NOUN

indeed soothe the savage _____.
                              NOUN

MAD LIBS® is fun to play with friends, but you can also play it by yourself! To begin with, DO NOT look at the story on the page below. Fill in the blanks on this page with the words called for. Then, using the words you have selected, fill in the blank spaces in the story.

Now you've created your own hilarious MAD LIBS® game!

LETTER TO A LOVELORN COLUMNIST

NUMBER _____

VERB ENDING IN "S" _____

VERB (PAST TENSE) _____

PLURAL NOUN _____

VERB _____

PLURAL NOUN _____

ADJECTIVE _____

PART OF THE BODY _____

ADJECTIVE _____

PERSON IN ROOM (FEMALE) _____

ADJECTIVE _____

VERB ENDING IN "ING" _____

VERB ENDING IN "ING" _____

PLURAL NOUN _____

VERB _____

SAME PLURAL NOUN _____

NUMBER _____

MAD LIBS®
LETTER TO A LOVELORN COLUMNIST

Dear Miss Lonelyhearts:

I've been engaged to the same man for _____ years. He
NUMBER

keeps telling me he _____ me, but we need to wait to get
VERB ENDING IN "S"

_____ until he makes more _____. If we
VERB (PAST TENSE)   PLURAL NOUN

marry now, we will have to _____ with my mother and eat
VERB

_____ every day. But isn't _____ love worth that?
PLURAL NOUN   ADJECTIVE

Should I put my _____ down and set a date, or just continue to
PART OF THE BODY

be _____?
ADJECTIVE

Signed, _____
PERSON IN ROOM (FEMALE)

Dear Young Lady:

Don't do anything _____. Something worth _____ is
ADJECTIVE   VERB ENDING IN "ING"

worth _____ for. I don't think eating _____ with
VERB ENDING IN "ING"   PLURAL NOUN

the man you _____ is bad, but eating _____ and
VERB   SAME PLURAL NOUN

living _____ miles away from your mother is better.
NUMBER

Signed, Miss Lonelyhearts

MAD LIBS® is fun to play with friends, but you can also play it by yourself! To begin with, DO NOT look at the story on the page below. Fill in the blanks on this page with the words called for. Then, using the words you have selected, fill in the blank spaces in the story.

Now you've created your own hilarious MAD LIBS® game!

FRANKENSTEIN, WHERE ARE YOU?

ADJECTIVE _____

ADJECTIVE _____

NUMBER _____

ADJECTIVE _____

PLURAL NOUN _____

PLURAL NOUN _____

PERSON IN ROOM _____

NOUN _____

ADJECTIVE _____

NUMBER _____

PLURAL NOUN _____

OCCUPATION _____

ADJECTIVE _____

NOUN _____

NOUN _____

ADJECTIVE _____

MAD LIBS®

FRANKENSTEIN, WHERE ARE YOU?

It is hard to believe that *Frankenstein*, one of the _____ horror
                                                              ADJECTIVE

stories of all time, was written by a very _____ woman. Mary
                                                   ADJECTIVE

Wollstonecraft Shelley was only _____ years old when she
                                        NUMBER

created this _____ masterpiece. Today this Gothic story has been
                    ADJECTIVE

made into a countless number of stage plays, as well as _____
                                                              PLURAL NOUN

and television _____. As a result of _____'s
                    PLURAL NOUN   PERSON IN ROOM

performance in the original _____, we think of Frankenstein as a
                                    NOUN

monster with a/an _____ head who is over _____
                         ADJECTIVE   NUMBER

feet tall and has _____ sticking out of his neck. We also believe
                        PLURAL NOUN

Frankenstein to be the name of the monster, when actually, it is the name of the

_____ who created him. Unfortunately, it was Dr. Frankenstein's
      OCCUPATION

_____ fate to be destroyed by the very _____
      ADJECTIVE   NOUN

he created. What we learn from this story is: You can't build your own

_____ without the _____ recipe.
      NOUN   ADJECTIVE

MAD LIBS® is fun to play with friends, but you can also play it by yourself! To begin with, DO NOT look at the story on the page below. Fill in the blanks on this page with the words called for. Then, using the words you have selected, fill in the blank spaces in the story.

Now you've created your own hilarious MAD LIBS® game!

LETTERS TO A TV EDITOR

PLURAL NOUN _____

ADJECTIVE _____

NOUN _____

ADJECTIVE _____

ADJECTIVE _____

NOUN _____

VERB _____

ADJECTIVE _____

ANIMAL (PLURAL) _____

NOUN _____

ADJECTIVE _____

VERB ENDING IN "ING" _____

NOUN _____

ADJECTIVE _____

PLURAL NOUN _____

ADJECTIVE _____

NOUN _____

NOUN _____

MAD LIBS®
LETTERS TO A TV EDITOR

How dumb can network _____ be? They cancel a/an _____
_____PLURAL NOUN_____ _____ADJECTIVE_____

show such as *I'll Be a Monkey's* _____ and replace it with
_____NOUN_____

another one of those _____ reality shows. Why don't they
_____ADJECTIVE_____

take all those _____ TV executives, put them on a desert
_____ADJECTIVE_____

_____, and leave them there to _____!
_____NOUN_____ _____VERB_____

Signed: A/An _____ Viewer
_____ADJECTIVE_____

Believe me, television is going to the _____. I can't believe
_____ANIMAL (PLURAL)_____

the _____ they're dishing out. What's being offered to the
_____NOUN_____

_____ public is truly mind-_____.
_____ADJECTIVE_____ _____VERB ENDING IN "ING"_____

Signed: A Disenchanted _____
_____NOUN_____

I think today's sitcoms are just as _____ as the golden _____
_____ADJECTIVE_____ _____PLURAL NOUN_____

of the past. What needs to be eliminated is the _____ laugh
_____ADJECTIVE_____

_____.
_____NOUN_____

Signed: A Confirmed Couch _____
_____NOUN_____

MAD LIBS® is fun to play with friends, but you can also play it by yourself! To begin with, DO NOT look at the story on the page below. Fill in the blanks on this page with the words called for. Then, using the words you have selected, fill in the blank spaces in the story.

Now you've created your own hilarious MAD LIBS® game!

INTRODUCTION

ADJECTIVE _____

ADJECTIVE _____

NOUN _____

VERB ENDING IN "ING" _____

PLURAL NOUN _____

PART OF THE BODY (PLURAL) _____

VERB ENDING IN "ING" _____

NOUN _____

PLURAL NOUN _____

PLURAL NOUN _____

PLURAL NOUN _____

NUMBER _____

NOUN _____

PART OF THE BODY _____

NOUN _____

ADVERB _____

NOUN _____

MAD LIBS®
INTRODUCTION

Once again, it is the time of year when parents can get rid of their

_____ kids by sending them to a/an _____
    ADJECTIVE   ADJECTIVE

summer camp. Today they are mostly "theme camps." There are football camps,

computer camps, _____ camps, _____ camps,
                           NOUN   VERB ENDING IN "ING"

and special camps for children who like to make ceramic _____
                                                                 PLURAL NOUN

with their _____. These camps have classes in
                         PART OF THE BODY (PLURAL)

_____ and in remedial _____. But all
    VERB ENDING IN "ING"   NOUN

summer, camps feed the kids _____ and make them sleep in
                                         PLURAL NOUN

_____ or rickety _____. Every kid has a counselor
    PLURAL NOUN   PLURAL NOUN

who is a big _____-year-old _____ who doesn't
                   NUMBER   NOUN

know his _____ from his _____. But kids
               PART OF THE BODY   NOUN

_____ put up with these indignities because they love camp and
    ADVERB

hate to go back to their own _____.
                                        NOUN

MAD LIBS® is fun to play with friends, but you can also play it by yourself! To begin with, DO NOT look at the story on the page below. Fill in the blanks on this page with the words called for. Then, using the words you have selected, fill in the blank spaces in the story.

Now you've created your own hilarious MAD LIBS® game!

ON MY SPECIAL DAY

PERSON IN ROOM _____

OCCUPATION _____

PERSON IN ROOM _____

NOUN _____

VERB _____

VERB _____

PLURAL NOUN _____

ADJECTIVE _____

PERSON IN ROOM _____

PERSON IN ROOM _____

PLURAL NOUN _____

PLURAL NOUN _____

CELEBRITY _____

CELEBRITY _____

PLURAL NOUN _____

NOUN _____

PERSON IN ROOM _____

A PLACE _____

NOUN _____

A PLACE _____

MAD LIBS®
ON MY SPECIAL DAY

The following is a list of historical events that tookplace on _____'s
$\qquad$ PERSON IN ROOM

birthday:

A/An _____ named _____ invented the
$\quad$ OCCUPATION $\qquad$ PERSON IN ROOM

_____, forever changing the way humans _____.
$\quad$ NOUN $\qquad$ VERB

Rock 'n' _____ band The _____ rose to the top of the
$\qquad$ VERB $\qquad$ PLURAL NOUN

music charts with their _____ hit song, "_____"
$\qquad$ ADJECTIVE $\qquad$ PERSON IN ROOM

_____ broke the record for the most _____ eaten
$\quad$ PERSON IN ROOM $\qquad$ PLURAL NOUN

in one sitting.

The film *The* _____, starring _____ and
$\qquad$ PLURAL NOUN $\qquad$ CELEBRITY

_____, opened nationwide, smashing box-office _____
$\quad$ CELEBRITY $\qquad$ PLURAL NOUN

around the _____.
$\qquad$ NOUN

_____, an explorer from (the) _____ became the
$\quad$ PERSON IN ROOM $\qquad$ A PLACE

first _____ to ever step foot in (the) _____.
$\qquad$ NOUN $\qquad$ A PLACE

MAD LIBS® is fun to play with friends, but you can also play it by yourself! To begin with, DO NOT look at the story on the page below. Fill in the blanks on this page with the words called for. Then, using the words you have selected, fill in the blank spaces in the story.

Now you've created your own hilarious MAD LIBS® game!

DOGS

NOUN _____

ADJECTIVE _____

ADJECTIVE _____

NOUN _____

NOUN _____

ADVERB _____

NOUN _____

NOUN _____

COLOR _____

ADJECTIVE _____

ADJECTIVE _____

NUMBER _____

ADJECTIVE _____

PLURAL NOUN _____

ADJECTIVE _____

NOUN _____

MAD LIBS®
DOGS

It has often been said that "a dog is man's best _____." Dogs are
                                                        NOUN

very _____ and can be taught many _____ tricks.
        ADJECTIVE   ADJECTIVE

A dog can be trained to carry a/an _____ in his mouth. And if you
                                          NOUN

throw this _____, he will run and fetch it. Dogs will also bark
                NOUN

_____ if someone tries to break into your _____
        ADVERB   NOUN

during the night. One of the most popular canine pets today is the

_____ Spaniel. Spaniels have curly _____ coats
        NOUN   COLOR

and _____ ears. They also have very _____
        ADJECTIVE   ADJECTIVE

dispositions and live to be _____ years old. Other popular dogs
                                    NUMBER

are _____ Terriers, German _____, and the
        ADJECTIVE   PLURAL NOUN

_____ Poodle. Every home should have a loyal dog for a/an
        ADJECTIVE

_____.
        NOUN

MAD LIBS® is fun to play with friends, but you can also play it by yourself! To begin with, DO NOT look at the story on the page below. Fill in the blanks on this page with the words called for. Then, using the words you have selected, fill in the blank spaces in the story.

Now you've created your own hilarious MAD LIBS® game!

THE SPOOKY OPERA, PART 1

NOUN _____

NOUN _____

NUMBER _____

CELEBRITY (MALE) _____

ADJECTIVE _____

ADJECTIVE _____

NOUN _____

NOUN _____

PERSON IN ROOM _____

ARTICLE OF CLOTHING _____

TYPE OF FOOD _____

PERSON IN ROOM (FEMALE) _____

ADJECTIVE _____

TYPE OF FOOD _____

TYPE OF LIQUID _____

MAD LIBS®

THE SPOOKY OPERA, PART 1

The _____ of the Opera was a silent _____ made
$\qquad$ NOUN $\qquad\qquad\qquad$ NOUN

_____ years ago, and it starred _____ as a/an
$\qquad$ NUMBER $\qquad\qquad\qquad$ CELEBRITY (MALE)

_____ monster who had formerly been a/an _____
ADJECTIVE $\qquad\qquad\qquad\qquad$ ADJECTIVE

singing _____ at the opera. But he got his face caught in a/an
$\qquad$ NOUN

_____ and when he recovered, he looked like _____.
NOUN $\qquad\qquad\qquad\qquad$ PERSON IN ROOM

So he hid in the tunnels beneath the opera house and wore a long

_____ and lived on dried beans and _____. One
ARTICLE OF CLOTHING $\qquad\qquad\qquad$ TYPE OF FOOD

day he saw _____ and fell in love with her. So he kidnapped
$\qquad$ PERSON IN ROOM (FEMALE)

her and took her to his _____ underground home. The monster
$\qquad\qquad\qquad$ ADJECTIVE

was nice to the girl and brought her delicious _____ and
$\qquad\qquad\qquad\qquad\qquad$ TYPE OF FOOD

_____.
TYPE OF LIQUID

MAD LIBS® is fun to play with friends, but you can also play it by yourself! To begin with, DO NOT look at the story on the page below. Fill in the blanks on this page with the words called for. Then, using the words you have selected, fill in the blank spaces in the story.

Now you've created your own hilarious MAD LIBS® game!

THE SPOOKY OPERA, PART 2

NOUN _____

NOUN _____

ADJECTIVE _____

NOUN _____

PART OF THE BODY _____

PERSON IN ROOM (MALE) _____

VERB ENDING IN "ING" _____

ADVERB _____

ADJECTIVE _____

NOUN _____

EXCLAMATION _____

VERB _____

NOUN _____

CELEBRITY (MALE) _____

ADVERB _____

NUMBER _____

Now that the monster had kidnapped the _____ he loved,
NOUN

he had to wear a/an _____ to cover his face because he
NOUN

was so _____. Naturally, the girl thought he was nothing
ADJECTIVE

but a/an _____ who was probably a little touched in the
NOUN

_____. Meanwhile, her fiancé, played by _____,
PART OF THE BODY   PERSON IN ROOM (MALE)

suspected what had happened and began _____ the
VERB ENDING IN "ING"

tunnels for her. But the monster had _____ prepared a/an
ADVERB

_____ trap, so when the fiancé went into the room, a huge
ADJECTIVE

_____ slammed down behind him.
NOUN

"_____!" the monster said to the girl. "Now you will have to marry
EXCLAMATION

me or I will _____ your fiancé."
VERB

"No, no!" the girl cried. "That would be a/an _____ worse than
NOUN

death!"

But the monster took off his mask and the girl saw that he looked just like

_____, so she married him. And they lived _____
CELEBRITY (MALE)   ADVERB

for _____ years.
NUMBER

MAD LIBS® is fun to play with friends, but you can also play it by yourself! To begin with, DO NOT look at the story on the page below. Fill in the blanks on this page with the words called for. Then, using the words you have selected, fill in the blank spaces in the story.

Now you've created your own hilarious MAD LIBS® game!

THE SPACE SHUTTLE

NOUN _____

PLURAL NOUN _____

VERB ENDING IN "ING" _____

PLURAL NOUN _____

A PLACE _____

PLURAL NOUN _____

ADJECTIVE _____

NOUN _____

NUMBER _____

NOUN _____

ADJECTIVE _____

VERB _____

VERB _____

PLURAL NOUN _____

VERB ENDING IN "ING" _____

NUMBER _____

ADVERB _____

NOUN _____

ADJECTIVE _____

MAD LIBS®
THE SPACE SHUTTLE

In 1981, the U.S. launched the first real space _____. It was

NOUN

named *Columbia* and was piloted by two brave _____.

PLURAL NOUN

They had practiced _____ for two years and were expert

VERB ENDING IN "ING"

_____. *Columbia* took off from (the) _____

PLURAL NOUN   A PLACE

using its powerful first-stage _____ and soared off into

PLURAL NOUN

the _____ blue _____. At an altitude of

ADJECTIVE   NOUN

_____ feet, it went into orbit around the _____.

NUMBER   NOUN

For people watching from Earth, it was a/an _____ sight to

ADJECTIVE

_____! Who could really _____ that there were

VERB   VERB

two _____ in space? It was mind-_____. After

PLURAL NOUN   VERB ENDING IN "ING"

_____ orbits, the shuttle landed _____ at an air

NUMBER   ADVERB

force _____. It was a/an _____ day for the U.S.

NOUN   ADJECTIVE

Space Program.

MAD LIBS® is fun to play with friends, but you can also play it by yourself! To begin with, DO NOT look at the story on the page below. Fill in the blanks on this page with the words called for. Then, using the words you have selected, fill in the blank spaces in the story.

Now you've created your own hilarious MAD LIBS® game!

DINOSAURS

ADJECTIVE _____

PLURAL NOUN _____

VERB (PAST TENSE) _____

A PLACE _____

NOUN _____

PLURAL NOUN _____

TYPE OF FOOD _____

FIRST NAME (MALE) _____

NOUN _____

PLURAL NOUN _____

TYPE OF FOOD _____

TYPE OF FOOD _____

PLURAL NOUN _____

MAD LIBS®
DINOSAURS

One hundred and fifty million years ago, the Earth was very _____.
ADJECTIVE

Huge _____, which were called dinosaurs, _____
PLURAL NOUN   VERB (PAST TENSE)

all over Europe and (the) _____. The biggest _____
A PLACE   NOUN

of all was called the brontosaurus. It weighed over 100 _____
PLURAL NOUN

and ate nothing but plants and _____. The most dangerous
TYPE OF FOOD

dinosaur was called tyrannosaurus _____. It was as tall as a two-
FIRST NAME (MALE)

story _____. It walked on its hind feet and its mouth was filled
NOUN

with hundreds of sharp, pointy _____. This dinosaur never ate
PLURAL NOUN

_____. It was a carnivore, and it only ate _____. It
TYPE OF FOOD   TYPE OF FOOD

is a good thing that all of these ferocious _____ are now extinct.
PLURAL NOUN

MAD LIBS® is fun to play with friends, but you can also play it by yourself! To begin with, DO NOT look at the story on the page below. Fill in the blanks on this page with the words called for. Then, using the words you have selected, fill in the blank spaces in the story.

Now you've created your own hilarious MAD LIBS® game!

MADISON AVENUE MAD LIBS

ADJECTIVE _____

A PLACE _____

VERB _____

ADJECTIVE _____

NOUN _____

VERB ENDING IN "ING" _____

ADVERB _____

NOUN _____

ADJECTIVE _____

PLURAL NOUN _____

NOUN _____

PLURAL NOUN _____

ADJECTIVE _____

ANIMAL _____

PLURAL NOUN _____

PLURAL NOUN _____

NUMBER _____

NOUN _____

PLURAL NOUN _____

NOUN _____

PLURAL NOUN _____

MAD LIBS®
MADISON AVENUE MAD LIBS

- _____ Express—don't leave (the) _____ without it.
  ADJECTIVE   A PLACE

- When you _____ enough to send the very _____.
                VERB   ADJECTIVE

- It's such a pleasure to take the _____ and leave the
                                        NOUN

_____ to us.
VERB ENDING IN "ING"

- Drive _____. The _____ you save may be your own.
        ADVERB   NOUN

- Is it live or is it _____?
                      ADJECTIVE

- Four out of five _____ recommend _____ for
                    PLURAL NOUN   NOUN

their _____ who chew gum.
      PLURAL NOUN

- _____ the _____ says, "Only you can prevent
  ADJECTIVE   ANIMAL

forest _____."
       PLURAL NOUN

- _____—no one can eat just _____.
  PLURAL NOUN   NUMBER

- Things go better with _____.
                        NOUN

- _____ melt in your _____, not in your _____.
  PLURAL NOUN   NOUN   PLURAL NOUN

MAD LIBS® is fun to play with friends, but you can also play it by yourself! To begin with, DO NOT look at the story on the page below. Fill in the blanks on this page with the words called for. Then, using the words you have selected, fill in the blank spaces in the story.

Now you've created your own hilarious MAD LIBS® game!

CHARLEMAGNE

ADJECTIVE _____

PLURAL NOUN _____

NOUN _____

ADJECTIVE _____

NOUN _____

NOUN _____

PLURAL NOUN _____

PLURAL NOUN _____

A PLACE _____

ADJECTIVE _____

PLURAL NOUN _____

ADJECTIVE _____

MAD LIBS
CHARLEMAGNE

Charlemagne was the _____ king of the Franks and
_____ ADJECTIVE

_____. In 800 AD, he was crowned Emperor of the Holy
PLURAL NOUN

Roman _____ by Pope Leo the Third. He was born in 742. His
NOUN

father was Pepin the _____, and his grandfather was Charles the
ADJECTIVE

_____. Charlemagne converted thousands of Saxons, who were
NOUN

_____ worshippers, to Christianity. He converted them by cutting
NOUN

off their _____ and setting fire to their _____.
PLURAL NOUN   PLURAL NOUN

In 778, he invaded Spain, but was defeated by the Moors at (the)

_____. Charlemagne was uneducated, but he had great
A PLACE

respect for education and established many _____ schools.
ADJECTIVE

And he was known for the justice of his _____ and his kindness to
PLURAL NOUN

_____ people.
ADJECTIVE

MAD LIBS® is fun to play with friends, but you can also play it by yourself! To begin with, DO NOT look at the story on the page below. Fill in the blanks on this page with the words called for. Then, using the words you have selected, fill in the blank spaces in the story.

Now you've created your own hilarious MAD LIBS® game!

HOW TO ENJOY YOURSELF ON THE BEACH

TYPE OF LIQUID _____

NOUN _____

PLURAL NOUN _____

ARTICLE OF CLOTHING _____

COLOR _____

PART OF THE BODY _____

PLURAL NOUN _____

ADJECTIVE _____

ADJECTIVE _____

PLURAL NOUN _____

ANIMAL _____

SILLY WORD _____

ADJECTIVE _____

ADVERB _____

MAD LIBS®
HOW TO ENJOY YOURSELF ON THE BEACH

When you go the beach, you must take along a big blanket, a thermos bottle

full of _____, lots of suntan _____, and a couple
          TYPE OF LIQUID   NOUN

of folding _____. Then you put on your _____
           PLURAL NOUN   ARTICLE OF CLOTHING

so you can get a beautiful _____ to last you all summer. You also
                           COLOR

should have a big hat to keep the sun off your _____. If you
                                               PART OF THE BODY

want exercise, you can find some _____ to play volleyball with.
                                 PLURAL NOUN

Volleyball is America's favorite _____ game. You can also bring
                                 ADJECTIVE

a/an _____ lunch, such as hard-boiled _____,
     ADJECTIVE   PLURAL NOUN

a few _____ sandwiches with mustard, and some bottles of
      ANIMAL

_____ cola. If you remember all of the above and get a place near
SILLY WORD

a/an _____ lifeguard, you can sunbathe _____ all day.
     ADJECTIVE   ADVERB

MAD LIBS® is fun to play with friends, but you can also play it by yourself! To begin with, DO NOT look at the story on the page below. Fill in the blanks on this page with the words called for. Then, using the words you have selected, fill in the blank spaces in the story.

Now you've created your own hilarious MAD LIBS® game!

HOT FUDGE SUNDAES

NOUN _____

NUMBER _____

PLURAL NOUN _____

ADJECTIVE _____

ADJECTIVE _____

ADJECTIVE _____

NOUN _____

NUMBER _____

PLURAL NOUN _____

NOUN _____

NOUN _____

NOUN _____

VERB (PAST TENSE) _____

PLURAL NOUN _____

ADJECTIVE _____

VERB _____

MAD LIBS®
HOT FUDGE SUNDAES

Making a hot fudge _____ is as simple as one, two, _____.
     NOUN   NUMBER

All you need are the following _____:
                                PLURAL NOUN

A pint of _____ ice cream
           ADJECTIVE

1 jar of _____ fudge sauce
          ADJECTIVE

1 cup of _____ nuts
          ADJECTIVE

1 can of whipped _____
                      NOUN

_____ maraschino _____
    NUMBER   PLURAL NOUN

Scoop the ice _____ into a glass _____. Pour on a
                 NOUN   NOUN

generous portion of hot _____ sauce, and add a heaping mound of
                             NOUN

_____ cream. Sprinkle with _____ and top off with
VERB (PAST TENSE)   PLURAL NOUN

a/an _____ cherry. Now _____ and enjoy!
       ADJECTIVE   VERB

MAD LIBS® is fun to play with friends, but you can also play it by yourself! To begin with, DO NOT look at the story on the page below. Fill in the blanks on this page with the words called for. Then, using the words you have selected, fill in the blank spaces in the story.

Now you've created your own hilarious MAD LIBS® game!

FAREWELL ADDRESS TO OUR CAMPING TRIP

PART OF THE BODY _____

NOUN _____

NUMBER _____

PLURAL NOUN _____

ADJECTIVE _____

NOUN _____

PLURAL NOUN _____

NOUN _____

NOUN _____

PLURAL NOUN _____

NOUN _____

NOUN _____

PLURAL NOUN _____

PLURAL NOUN _____

PART OF THE BODY (PLURAL) _____

VERB ENDING IN "ING" _____

MAD LIBS®

FAREWELL ADDRESS TO OUR CAMPING TRIP

Everyone in this family needs to have his or her _____ examined.
PART OF THE BODY

Why are we going on another camping trip? Am I the only one who remembers

last year? On our way to the camp _____, we had not one but
NOUN

_____ flat _____. Then, after we pitched our tent,
NUMBER   PLURAL NOUN

a/an _____ grizzly _____ trashed it, tore it
ADJECTIVE   NOUN

into little _____, and stared at us as he ate every morsel of
PLURAL NOUN

our first night's _____. We got by without our tent by building
NOUN

a roaring _____ and sleeping in the open air under a blanket of
NOUN

twinkling _____. But no sooner had we fallen asleep than there
PLURAL NOUN

was a sudden bolt of _____ and a clap of _____,
NOUN   NOUN

and it started raining cats and _____. By the time the morning
PLURAL NOUN

came we were wet and loaded with mosquito _____ on our
PLURAL NOUN

_____. Okay, now that I've refreshed your memory, do you still
PART OF THE BODY (PLURAL)

want to go _____? You do? Go ahead, see if I care. Wait, I'm
VERB ENDING IN "ING"

coming.

MAD LIBS® is fun to play with friends, but you can also play it by yourself! To begin with, DO NOT look at the story on the page below. Fill in the blanks on this page with the words called for. Then, using the words you have selected, fill in the blank spaces in the story.

Now you've created your own hilarious MAD LIBS® game!

A HISTORY OF PIRATE LADS

COLOR _____

ADJECTIVE _____

NOUN _____

NOUN _____

PLURAL NOUN _____

PLURAL NOUN _____

VERB _____

NOUN _____

PERSON IN ROOM (FEMALE) _____

NOUN _____

NOUN _____

PLURAL NOUN _____

NOUN _____

NOUN _____

NOUN _____

NOUN _____

PLURAL NOUN _____

ADJECTIVE _____

MAD LIBS®
A HISTORY OF PIRATE LADS

Pretending to be a pirate is fun, but did you know that there were real pirates

who sailed the ocean _____? Have you heard of Edward
                              COLOR

"Blackbeard" Teach? He was a/an _____ pirate with a long
                                          ADJECTIVE

black _____ that covered most of his _____.
            NOUN   NOUN

He would weave _____ into it and set them on fire to strike
                  PLURAL NOUN

fear in his enemies' _____ Another pirate, Francis Drake,
                          PLURAL NOUN

taught himself to _____. He learned every reef and
                              VERB

_____ in the Caribbean, and Queen _____
        NOUN   PERSON IN ROOM (FEMALE)

made him a/an _____ of the royal _____. She
                      NOUN   NOUN

even knighted him for his bravery and remarkable _____! Captain
                                                      PLURAL NOUN

Henry Morgan has a similar _____. He became a commander of
                                    NOUN

the English _____! Then there was William Kidd, whose pirate
                  NOUN

_____ was called *The Adventure* _____. At
        NOUN   NOUN

first, Kidd was reluctant to become a pirate and start pillaging and plundering

_____ but he ended up becoming a very successful, if
      PLURAL NOUN

_____, pirate.
    ADJECTIVE

MAD LIBS® is fun to play with friends, but you can also play it by yourself! To begin with, DO NOT look at the story on the page below. Fill in the blanks on this page with the words called for. Then, using the words you have selected, fill in the blank spaces in the story.

Now you've created your own hilarious MAD LIBS® game!

A HISTORY OF PIRATE LADIES

VERB (PAST TENSE) _____

ADJECTIVE _____

VERB (PAST TENSE) _____

VERB _____

ADJECTIVE _____

PLURAL NOUN _____

ADJECTIVE _____

NOUN _____

ADJECTIVE _____

ADVERB _____

NOUN _____

VERB (PAST TENSE) _____

NOUN _____

PLURAL NOUN _____

PLURAL NOUN _____

NOUN _____

ADJECTIVE _____

A PLACE _____

PLURAL NOUN _____

MAD LIBS®
A HISTORY OF PIRATE LADIES

Now that you know about the male pirates who _____ on the

VERB (PAST TENSE)

seven seas, you should learn a little about the _____ ladies

ADJECTIVE

who also _____ and plundered. Generally, women weren't

VERB (PAST TENSE)

allowed to _____ on pirate ships, but that didn't stop them.

VERB

They found ways to fool those _____ _____!

ADJECTIVE PLURAL NOUN

First there was Anne Bonny, a/an _____ young _____

ADJECTIVE NOUN

of _____ strength who had a reputation for being

ADJECTIVE

_____ handy with a/an _____. Then there was Mary

ADVERB NOUN

Read, who _____ with Anne on the same _____!

VERB (PAST TENSE) NOUN

Both of these female _____ dressed like _____ to

PLURAL NOUN PLURAL NOUN

disguise themselves aboard the _____ *The Revenge*. Then there

NOUN

was Grace O'Malley—who wasn't just a pirate captain, but a/an _____

ADJECTIVE

chieftain in (the) _____, too! So you see, anything that

A PLACE

_____ could do, these women could do better!

PLURAL NOUN

MAD LIBS® is fun to play with friends, but you can also play it by yourself! To begin with, DO NOT look at the story on the page below. Fill in the blanks on this page with the words called for. Then, using the words you have selected, fill in the blank spaces in the story.

Now you've created your own hilarious MAD LIBS® game!

GOOD HEALTH TO ONE AND ALL

ADJECTIVE _____

ADJECTIVE _____

VERB ENDING IN "ING" _____

PART OF THE BODY (PLURAL) _____

PLURAL NOUN _____

PLURAL NOUN _____

NOUN _____

PLURAL NOUN _____

PLURAL NOUN _____

NOUN _____

PLURAL NOUN _____

PLURAL NOUN _____

ADJECTIVE _____

PLURAL NOUN _____

ADJECTIVE _____

ADJECTIVE _____

MAD LIBS®

GOOD HEALTH TO ONE AND ALL

A/An _____ fitness revolution is taking place. Today, millions of
        ADJECTIVE

people are doing all kinds of _____ exercises such as jogging,
                        ADJECTIVE

walking, and _____ to get their _____ in
            VERB ENDING IN "ING"   PART OF THE BODY (PLURAL)

shape and develop their _____. Many go to gyms and health
                        PLURAL NOUN

_____ to work out by punching a/an _____,
    PLURAL NOUN   NOUN

lifting _____, or performing aerobic _____. In
        PLURAL NOUN   PLURAL NOUN

the past _____ people have become very weight-conscious. They
            NOUN

have learned what _____ they should and should not eat. They
                    PLURAL NOUN

know it's healthy to eat green _____ and _____
                                PLURAL NOUN   ADJECTIVE

fruit. They also know to avoid foods high in _____
                                                PLURAL NOUN

and _____ fats, especially if they want to lead a long and
        ADJECTIVE

_____ life.
    ADJECTIVE

MAD LIBS® is fun to play with friends, but you can also play it by yourself! To begin with, DO NOT look at the story on the page below. Fill in the blanks on this page with the words called for. Then, using the words you have selected, fill in the blank spaces in the story.

Now you've created your own hilarious MAD LIBS® game!

TAKE ME OUT TO THE BALL GAME!

NOUN _____

NOUN _____

NOUN _____

NOUN _____

PLURAL NOUN _____

PLURAL NOUN _____

ADJECTIVE _____

SILLY WORD _____

NOUN _____

PLURAL NOUN _____

NOUN _____

NOUN _____

NOUN _____

PLURAL NOUN _____

NOUN _____

NOUN _____

NOUN _____

VERB (PAST TENSE) _____

MAD LIBS®
TAKE ME OUT TO THE BALL GAME!

It's always great to attend a baseball _____, but it's an extra
                                        NOUN

special _____ to go with our grandfather. He's been a permanent
         NOUN

_____ at the park since he was just a wee _____.
        NOUN   NOUN

Everyone there knows him, including the _____ who sell hot,
                                          PLURAL NOUN

roasted _____ and even the _____ umpires. They
         PLURAL NOUN   ADJECTIVE

all greet him with "Hiya, _____," which was Grandpa's nickname
                           SILLLY WORD

when he was a little _____. We all thought that Grandpa's
                      NOUN

season _____, located behind home _____,
        PLURAL NOUN   NOUN

were the best in the ballpark until our family was invited to sit in the owners'

_____ to celebrate Grandpa's seventy-fifth birthday. It was so
        NOUN

exciting! As the organist played "Happy _____ to You" and
                                          NOUN

fifty thousand _____ sang along, Grandpa was escorted to the
                PLURAL NOUN

pitcher's _____ to throw out the first _____.
           NOUN   NOUN

Everyone in the _____-park _____, but our
                 NOUN   VERB (PAST TENSE)

family was by far the loudest.

MAD LIBS® is fun to play with friends, but you can also play it by yourself! To begin with, DO NOT look at the story on the page below. Fill in the blanks on this page with the words called for. Then, using the words you have selected, fill in the blank spaces in the story.

Now you've created your own hilarious MAD LIBS® game!

BOWLING

ADJECTIVE _____

ADJECTIVE _____

ADJECTIVE _____

PLURAL NOUN _____

NUMBER _____

NOUN _____

NOUN _____

PLURAL NOUN _____

NOUN _____

NOUN _____

ADJECTIVE _____

NOUN _____

ADJECTIVE _____

ADJECTIVE _____

NOUN _____

ADJECTIVE _____

NOUN _____

MAD LIBS®
BOWLING

Bowling is a game in which a/an _____ ball is rolled along a/an
                                    ADJECTIVE

_____ lane in an attempt to knock over _____
        ADJECTIVE   ADJECTIVE

wooden _____. If you knock over all _____ pins
           PLURAL NOUN   NUMBER

with your first _____, you have made a/an _____.
                    NOUN   NOUN

If it takes two balls to knock down all the _____, you've
                                                PLURAL NOUN

scored a/an _____. If you ever bowl 300, which is the perfect
                NOUN

_____, you can expect to be interviewed by _____
      NOUN   ADJECTIVE

sportswriters and have your _____ in the _____
                                NOUN   ADJECTIVE

newspaper. Bowling is _____ fun for every member of your
                          ADJECTIVE

_____ and it is also _____ exercise for developing
      NOUN   ADJECTIVE

your _____.
          NOUN

MAD LIBS® is fun to play with friends, but you can also play it by yourself! To begin with, DO NOT look at the story on the page below. Fill in the blanks on this page with the words called for. Then, using the words you have selected, fill in the blank spaces in the story.

Now you've created your own hilarious MAD LIBS® game!

WHEN I GROW UP

NUMBER _____

VERB ENDING IN "ING" _____

NOUN _____

LAST NAME _____

VERB ENDING IN "ING" _____

ADVERB _____

OCCUPATION _____

OCCUPATION _____

ADJECTIVE _____

NUMBER _____

A PLACE _____

PLURAL NOUN _____

NUMBER _____

NOUN _____

A PLACE _____

PLURAL NOUN _____

NOUN _____

ADJECTIVE _____

VERB ENDING IN "ING" _____

MAD LIBS®
WHEN I GROW UP

Now that I've graduated from grade _____, I'm going to start
                                            NUMBER

_____ more often. After all, I'm practically a/an _____!
VERB ENDING IN "ING"   NOUN

Since I want to be just like Donald _____ when I grow
                                            LAST NAME

up, I'd better start _____ as _____ as possible.
                     VERB ENDING IN "ING"   ADVERB

I think this summer I'm going to get a part-time job as a/an _____
                                                                OCCUPATION

or a/an _____.That will teach me how to be _____
            OCCUPATION   ADJECTIVE

and maybe I'll even make _____ dollars! Then I can put all of my
                              NUMBER

money in (the) _____ and collect _____. When
                  A PLACE   PLURAL NOUN

I retire at age _____, I'll be a/an _____. Maybe
                    NUMBER   NOUN

I'll even get to live on the beach in (the) _____, buy expensive
                                                A PLACE

_____, and drive a fancy _____. Wouldn't that be
    PLURAL NOUN   NOUN

_____? I'd better start _____ right away!
    ADJECTIVE   VERB ENDING IN "ING"

MAD LIBS® is fun to play with friends, but you can also play it by yourself! To begin with, DO NOT look at the story on the page below. Fill in the blanks on this page with the words called for. Then, using the words you have selected, fill in the blank spaces in the story.

Now you've created your own hilarious MAD LIBS® game!

GREAT EXCUSES FOR BEING LATE

ADJECTIVE _____

PERSON IN ROOM _____

ADJECTIVE _____

PART OF THE BODY _____

NOUN _____

NOUN _____

NUMBER _____

PLURAL NOUN _____

TYPE OF LIQUID _____

ADVERB _____

PERSON IN ROOM _____

ADJECTIVE _____

ADJECTIVE _____

ADJECTIVE _____

ADJECTIVE _____

ADJECTIVE _____

PLURAL NOUN _____

NOUN _____

PLURAL NOUN _____

PLURAL NOUN _____

MAD LIBS®
GREAT EXCUSES FOR BEING LATE

Dear Physical Education Teacher,

Please excuse my son/daughter from missing _____ class
ADJECTIVE

yesterday. When _____ awakened yesterday, I could see that
PERSON IN ROOM

his/her nose was _____. He/She also complained of
ADJECTIVE

_____ aches and having a sore _____, and I took
PART OF THE BODY   NOUN

him/her to the family _____. The doctor quickly diagnosed it to be
NOUN

the _____-hour flu and suggested he/she take two _____
NUMBER   PLURAL NOUN

with a glass of _____ and go to bed _____.
TYPE OF LIQUID   ADVERB

Dear Science Teacher,

Please excuse _____ for being late for your _____
PERSON IN ROOM   ADJECTIVE

science class. It's my fault. I feel _____. He/She was
ADJECTIVE

up until the _____ hours of the morning completing his/her
ADJECTIVE

_____ project. Just as he/she was going out of the _____
ADJECTIVE   ADJECTIVE

door, I noticed that his/her only pair of _____ had a/an
PLURAL NOUN

_____ in them. It took me an hour to find my _____,
NOUN   PLURAL NOUN

enabling me to sew his/her _____ back together.
PLURAL NOUN

MAD LIBS® is fun to play with friends, but you can also play it by yourself! To begin with, DO NOT look at the story on the page below. Fill in the blanks on this page with the words called for. Then, using the words you have selected, fill in the blank spaces in the story.

Now you've created your own hilarious MAD LIBS® game!

MORE GREAT EXCUSES FOR TARDINESS

ADJECTIVE _____

PERSON IN ROOM _____

ADJECTIVE _____

ANIMAL _____

ADJECTIVE _____

NUMBER _____

PART OF THE BODY (PLURAL) _____

PERSON IN ROOM _____

PLURAL NOUN _____

NOUN _____

NOUN _____

ADJECTIVE _____

VERB (PAST TENSE) _____

NOUN _____

NOUN _____

ADJECTIVE _____

Dear Principal,

I am sorry to have to tell you that my _____ son/daughter,

ADJECTIVE

_____, will be unable to attend your _____ school

PERSON IN ROOM ADJECTIVE

this week as he/she has caught a case of the _____ pox. The

ANIMAL

_____ doctor says that it will be _____ weeks

ADJECTIVE NUMBER

before he/she is healthy and back on his/her _____ again.

PART OF THE BODY (PLURAL)

Dear Math Teacher,

I was driving _____ to school when the _____

PERSON IN ROOM PLURAL NOUN

failed and my car crashed into a/an _____. By the time the

NOUN

tow _____ finally arrived and the _____

NOUN ADJECTIVE

mechanic _____ the _____ and recharged the

VERB (PAST TENSE) NOUN

_____, we had missed your _____ class.

NOUN ADJECTIVE

MAD LIBS® is fun to play with friends, but you can also play it by yourself! To begin with, DO NOT look at the story on the page below. Fill in the blanks on this page with the words called for. Then, using the words you have selected, fill in the blank spaces in the story.

Now you've created your own hilarious MAD LIBS® game!

PAGES FROM A MARTIAN GIFT CATALOG

ADJECTIVE _____

NOUN _____

PLURAL NOUN _____

ADJECTIVE _____

NOUN _____

TYPE OF LIQUID _____

NUMBER _____

PLURAL NOUN _____

NOUN _____

PLURAL NOUN _____

PLURAL NOUN _____

ADVERB _____

PART OF THE BODY _____

NOUN _____

PLURAL NOUN _____

NOUN _____

ADJECTIVE _____

PLURAL NOUN _____

MAD LIBS®
PAGES FROM A MARTIAN GIFT CATALOG

Here is a really _____ bargain in solid _____
                        ADJECTIVE   NOUN

_____. These handsome but _____ gifts can be
      PLURAL NOUN   ADJECTIVE

used to hold down your _____ while you're having your morning
                              NOUN

cup of _____. Guaranteed for _____ eons and
           TYPE OF LIQUID   NUMBER

only fourteen gold _____ each.
                         PLURAL NOUN

Dress up your _____ with one of these folding _____.
                    NOUN   PLURAL NOUN

Comes with white enamel _____ and is delivered _____
                               PLURAL NOUN   ADVERB

by Arcturian Express. Completely assembled except for the _____
                                                               PART OF THE BODY

rest which is easily installed with a/an _____ and some
                                               NOUN

_____.
      PLURAL NOUN

A most welcome gift for the _____ season that will bring hours
                                  NOUN

of happiness to you and your _____ little _____.
                                   ADJECTIVE   PLURAL NOUN

MAD LIBS® is fun to play with friends, but you can also play it by yourself! To begin with, DO NOT look at the story on the page below. Fill in the blanks on this page with the words called for. Then, using the words you have selected, fill in the blank spaces in the story.

Now you've created your own hilarious MAD LIBS® game!

RULES FOR A SNOWBALL FIGHT

ADJECTIVE _____

VERB ENDING IN "ING" _____

NOUN _____

PLURAL NOUN _____

PLURAL NOUN _____

NOUN _____

PLURAL NOUN _____

PART OF THE BODY _____

NOUN _____

PLURAL NOUN _____

PLURAL NOUN _____

ADVERB _____

ADJECTIVE _____

NOUN _____

PLURAL NOUN _____

ADJECTIVE _____

NOUN _____

NOUN _____

MAD LIBS®
RULES FOR A SNOWBALL FIGHT

The _____ winter games committee does not recognize snowball
       ADJECTIVE

_____ as an official _____. Nevertheless, it has
VERB ENDING IN "ING"   NOUN

established rules and _____ for the athletes who want to throw
                          PLURAL NOUN

icy _____ at one another.
      PLURAL NOUN

• Contestants can toss only one _____ at a time and from a
                                    NOUN

distance of not less than twenty-five _____ away.
                                          PLURAL NOUN

• Aiming at a/an _____ is not permitted. If anybody is hit below
                 PART OF THE BODY

the _____, that person automatically wins.
        NOUN

• Loading a snowball with heavy _____ or solid _____
                                   PLURAL NOUN   PLURAL NOUN

is _____ forbidden. Snowball tampering will result in
        ADVERB

_____ penalties or rejection from the _____.
   ADJECTIVE   NOUN

• All _____ must wear _____ gear that protects
         PLURAL NOUN   ADJECTIVE

their eyes, as well as their _____ and _____.
                                NOUN   NOUN

MAD LIBS® is fun to play with friends, but you can also play it by yourself! To begin with, DO NOT look at the story on the page below. Fill in the blanks on this page with the words called for. Then, using the words you have selected, fill in the blank spaces in the story.

Now you've created your own hilarious MAD LIBS® game!

PILOT TO PASSENGERS

ADJECTIVE _____

CELEBRITY _____

NOUN _____

ADJECTIVE _____

VERB ENDING IN "ING" _____

A PLACE _____

NUMBER _____

NUMBER _____

TYPE OF LIQUID _____

ADJECTIVE _____

NOUN _____

VERB _____

ADJECTIVE _____

NOUN _____

ADJECTIVE _____

VERB _____

ADJECTIVE _____

ADJECTIVE _____

MAD LIBS®
PILOT TO PASSENGERS

Ladies and gentlemen, welcome aboard _____ Airlines flight 750.
_____ADJECTIVE_____

This is your captain and pilot, _____. The plane you are traveling
_____CELEBRITY_____

on is the latest Strato-_____, with four _____
_____NOUN_____ADJECTIVE

engines. At present, we are _____ directly over (the)
_____VERB ENDING "ING"_____

_____. Our speed is _____ miles per hour, and
____A PLACE_____NUMBER

we are flying at an altitude of _____ feet. If you care for a cup of
_____NUMBER

_____ or a/an _____ sandwich, please push the
___TYPE OF LIQUID_____ADJECTIVE

_____ located over your seat, and our flight attendant will be glad
____NOUN

to _____ you. We have a/an _____ tailwind and
_____VERB_____ADJECTIVE

will soon be flying through a heavy _____ storm. So I'll have to
_____NOUN

ask you all to fasten your _____ belts and _____
_____ADJECTIVE_____VERB

your trays to the _____ position. In the meantime, I hope you
_____ADJECTIVE

have a/an _____ trip.
_____ADJECTIVE

MAD LIBS® is fun to play with friends, but you can also play it by yourself! To begin with, DO NOT look at the story on the page below. Fill in the blanks on this page with the words called for. Then, using the words you have selected, fill in the blank spaces in the story.

Now you've created your own hilarious MAD LIBS® game!

HOW TO CLEAN YOUR COMPUTER

ADJECTIVE _____

ADVERB _____

VERB _____

NUMBER _____

ADJECTIVE _____

NOUN _____

A PLACE _____

ADVERB _____

PLURAL NOUN _____

TYPE OF LIQUID _____

ADJECTIVE _____

PERSON IN ROOM (MALE) _____

ADJECTIVE _____

TYPE OF FOOD (PLURAL) _____

EXCLAMATION _____

PART OF THE BODY _____

VERB ENDING IN "ING" _____

VERB ENDING IN "ING" _____

NOUN _____

ADJECTIVE _____

MAD LIBS®
HOW TO CLEAN YOUR COMPUTER

Since I use my computer every day, it can get _____ really
                                                    ADJECTIVE

_____. I always make sure to _____ it every
        ADVERB   VERB

_____ days in order to keep it shiny and _____.
    NUMBER   ADJECTIVE

I'll grab a soft _____ from (the) _____ and
                        NOUN   A PLACE

_____ wipe the keyboard down to get rid of all the _____.
    ADVERB   PLURAL NOUN

Then I squirt some _____ on the screen to get it nice and
                        TYPE OF LIQUID

_____. This week, it was extra dirty because my little brother
        ADJECTIVE

_____ decided to bring his _____ plate
   PERSON IN ROOM (MALE)   ADJECTIVE

of _____ into my room and eat it at my desk. When I yelled
   TYPE OF FOOD (PLURAL)

_____ and told him to stop, he stuck out his _____
     EXCLAMATION   PART OF THE BODY

at me and continued _____. Then he started _____
                      VERB ENDING IN "ING"   VERB ENDING IN "ING"

so hard that he spilled all of his food all over my _____. That is the
                                                            NOUN

last time I'll let my _____ little brother in my room ever again!
                            ADJECTIVE

MAD LIBS® is fun to play with friends, but you can also play it by yourself! To begin with, DO NOT look at the story on the page below. Fill in the blanks on this page with the words called for. Then, using the words you have selected, fill in the blank spaces in the story.

Now you've created your own hilarious MAD LIBS® game!

LETTERS PARENTS HOPE GOT LOST IN THE MAIL

ADVERB _____

NOUN _____

NOUN _____

ADJECTIVE _____

COLOR _____

NOUN _____

PART OF THE BODY _____

NOUN _____

ADJECTIVE _____

PERSON IN ROOM (FEMALE) _____

NOUN _____

PLURAL NOUN _____

ADJECTIVE _____

NOUN _____

PART OF THE BODY _____

NUMBER _____

NOUN _____

ADJECTIVE _____

PERSON IN ROOM (MALE) _____

MAD LIBS®

LETTERS PARENTS HOPE GOT LOST IN THE MAIL

Dear Folks,

I'm in L.A. It is _____ awesome. Yesterday, I met the greatest
                        ADVERB

_____. He plays _____ with a/an _____
      NOUN   NOUN   ADJECTIVE

band. He has _____ hair and wears a/an _____ in
                   COLOR   NOUN

his _____. He's the _____ of my dreams.
      PART OF THE BODY   NOUN

   Your _____ daughter, _____
              ADJECTIVE   PERSON IN ROOM (FEMALE)

Dear Folks,

Please send money. I found a really great surf-_____ for only
                                                        NOUN

150 _____. I borrowed the money from my _____
        PLURAL NOUN   ADJECTIVE

girlfriend, who is a life-_____ at the beach and is teaching me
                                NOUN

to surf nine-_____ waves. Although she is _____
                  PART OF THE BODY   NUMBER

years older than I am, I know she's the right _____ for me.
                                                        NOUN

   Your _____ son, _____
              ADJECTIVE   PERSON IN ROOM (MALE)

MAD LIBS® is fun to play with friends, but you can also play it by yourself! To begin with, DO NOT look at the story on the page below. Fill in the blanks on this page with the words called for. Then, using the words you have selected, fill in the blank spaces in the story.

Now you've created your own hilarious MAD LIBS® game!

FOURTH OF JULY

NOUN _____

NOUN _____

ADJECTIVE _____

NOUN _____

NOUN _____

ADJECTIVE _____

PLURAL NOUN _____

PLURAL NOUN _____

PLURAL NOUN _____

ADJECTIVE _____

NOUN _____

NOUN _____

NOUN _____

PLURAL NOUN _____

PLURAL NOUN _____

PLURAL NOUN _____

ADJECTIVE _____

ADVERB _____

VERB _____

PLURAL NOUN _____

NOUN _____

MAD LIBS®
FOURTH OF JULY

Every year on the _____ of July, we celebrate Independence
NOUN

Day. This holiday commemorates the birth of our _____.
NOUN

Many _____ citizens observe Independence _____
ADJECTIVE   NOUN

by hanging their _____ from a window or by running it up
NOUN

a/an _____ pole. Most _____ spend this
ADJECTIVE   PLURAL NOUN

holiday at home with family and _____ or visit national
PLURAL NOUN

_____ or _____ beaches. Food as
PLURAL NOUN   ADJECTIVE

American as apple _____, hamburgers, and corn on the
NOUN

_____ are traditional holiday _____.
NOUN   NOUN

And in the evening, there are displays of _____ such as Roman
PLURAL NOUN

_____, shooting _____, and _____
PLURAL NOUN   PLURAL NOUN   ADJECTIVE

rockets that _____ _____ through the sky. A
ADVERB   VERB

word of caution: Do not use _____ unless you are supervised
PLURAL NOUN

by a knowledgeable _____.
NOUN

MAD LIBS® is fun to play with friends, but you can also play it by yourself! To begin with, DO NOT look at the story on the page below. Fill in the blanks on this page with the words called for. Then, using the words you have selected, fill in the blank spaces in the story.

Now you've created your own hilarious MAD LIBS® game!

HOW TO WRITE A LOVE LETTER

NOUN _____

NOUN _____

NOUN _____

NOUN _____

ADVERB _____

PLURAL NOUN _____

NOUN _____

NOUN _____

NOUN _____

ADJECTIVE _____

VERB _____

ADVERB _____

NOUN _____

ADJECTIVE _____

NOUN _____

ADVERB _____

NOUN _____

MAD LIBS®

HOW TO WRITE A LOVE LETTER

If you want to send an easy-to-read letter, fax, or e-_____ to a
_____ **NOUN**

loved _____, a dear _____, or even a business
_____ **NOUN** _____ **NOUN**

_____, you must know how to punctuate it _____!
NOUN **ADVERB**

Follow these easily understood _____ for the proper placement
PLURAL NOUN

of a period, a comma, a question _____, or an exclamation
NOUN

_____, and you'll have it made.
NOUN

A period only comes at the end of a/an _____.
NOUN

A comma is a/an _____ pause in a sentence. It separates words
ADJECTIVE

that would be confused if they _____ together.
VERB

The question mark is _____ used after a/an _____
ADVERB **NOUN**

is asked.

The exclamation mark tells the reader that what has just been written is

urgent, significant, and _____. It only comes at the end of a/an
ADJECTIVE

_____. Now you are _____ equipped to write an
NOUN **ADVERB**

easily understood love _____.
NOUN

MAD LIBS® is fun to play with friends, but you can also play it by yourself! To begin with, DO NOT look at the story on the page below. Fill in the blanks on this page with the words called for. Then, using the words you have selected, fill in the blank spaces in the story.

Now you've created your own hilarious MAD LIBS® game!

KITCHEN INSPECTION

PLURAL NOUN _____

ADJECTIVE _____

ADJECTIVE _____

PART OF THE BODY (PLURAL) _____

ADJECTIVE _____

ANIMAL (PLURAL) _____

ANIMAL (PLURAL) _____

PLURAL NOUN _____

CELEBRITY _____

NOUN _____

NOUN _____

NOUN _____

NOUN _____

TYPE OF LIQUID _____

PLURAL NOUN _____

NOUN _____

PLURAL NOUN _____

PLURAL NOUN _____

ADJECTIVE _____

MAD LIBS®
KITCHEN INSPECTION

Inspectors from the State Department of Health and _____ came
PLURAL NOUN

here today to inspect the _____ kitchen and to make sure that
ADJECTIVE

our _____ cooks were washing their _____
ADJECTIVE   PART OF THE BODY (PLURAL)

before preparing our _____ meals. And that there are no little
ADJECTIVE

_____ or _____ running around in the kitchen
ANIMAL (PLURAL)   ANIMAL (PLURAL)

and spreading _____. They checked the lunch prepared by our
PLURAL NOUN

dietician, _____. We had spaghetti and _____ balls.
CELEBRITY   NOUN

On Tuesdays, we have boiled _____ with rice. On Wednesdays, we
NOUN

have a choice of _____ soup or a/an _____ omelet
NOUN   NOUN

with _____ sauce. The inspector found a lot of _____
TYPE OF LIQUID   PLURAL NOUN

in the salad and said there was too much _____ in the milk. In the
NOUN

future, we will have fewer _____ to eat and more _____.
PLURAL NOUN   PLURAL NOUN

But I bet it will still taste _____.
ADJECTIVE

MAD LIBS® is fun to play with friends, but you can also play it by yourself! To begin with, DO NOT look at the story on the page below. Fill in the blanks on this page with the words called for. Then, using the words you have selected, fill in the blank spaces in the story.

Now you've created your own hilarious MAD LIBS® game!

TOYS FOR THE KIDS

ADJECTIVE _____

PLURAL NOUN _____

ADJECTIVE _____

SILLY WORD _____

PLURAL NOUN _____

NUMBER _____

VERB _____

NOUN _____

PLURAL NOUN _____

NOUN _____

ADJECTIVE _____

NOUN _____

NOUN _____

ADJECTIVE _____

ADJECTIVE _____

ADJECTIVE _____

PLURAL NOUN _____

Today's parents buy very _____ toys for their little
<u>ADJECTIVE</u>

_____. Fifty years ago, children got _____
<u>PLURAL NOUN</u>   <u>ADJECTIVE</u>

electric trains or baby dolls that said "_____" when you
<u>SILLY WORD</u>

squeezed them. Now children only want electronic _____.
<u>PLURAL NOUN</u>

Even _____-year-olds know how to _____
<u>NUMBER</u>   <u>VERB</u>

on a computer or a/an _____ processor. Kids want remote-
<u>NOUN</u>

controlled _____. Or tiny robot monsters that can blow up your
<u>PLURAL NOUN</u>

_____ or take you _____ prisoner. Everything
<u>NOUN</u>   <u>ADJECTIVE</u>

has to have a silicon _____ in it and be operated by a nine-volt
<u>NOUN</u>

_____. By the year 2010, all American children will probably want
<u>NOUN</u>

to have their own _____ space shuttle and _____
<u>ADJECTIVE</u>   <u>ADJECTIVE</u>

robot playmate manufactured by General Motors. In fact, by that time, maybe

children will be manufactured by a/an _____ assembly line and
<u>ADJECTIVE</u>

operated by nine-volt _____.
<u>PLURAL NOUN</u>

MAD LIBS® is fun to play with friends, but you can also play it by yourself! To begin with, DO NOT look at the story on the page below. Fill in the blanks on this page with the words called for. Then, using the words you have selected, fill in the blank spaces in the story.

Now you've created your own hilarious MAD LIBS® game!

MAD LIBS RECORD OFFER

PLURAL NOUN _____

NOUN _____

ADJECTIVE _____

PLURAL NOUN _____

ADJECTIVE _____

PERSON IN ROOM _____

NUMBER _____

NOUN _____

PART OF THE BODY _____

VERB ENDING IN "ING" _____

NOUN _____

NOUN _____

PERSON IN ROOM (MALE) _____

ADJECTIVE _____

ADJECTIVE _____

MAD LIBS

MAD LIBS RECORD OFFER

Ladies and _____ of the TV audience, before we return to our late,
PLURAL NOUN

late _____, I want to tell you about a/an _____
NOUN   ADJECTIVE

musical offer. For only five dollars and ninety-five _____, you
PLURAL NOUN

can now get all of the _____ hits that _____
ADJECTIVE   PERSON IN ROOM

has put out over the past _____ years. This album is on a four-
NUMBER

track _____ and features such hits as "Raindrops Are Falling On My
NOUN

_____" and "_____ May Be Dangerous to Your
PART OF THE BODY   VERB ENDING IN "ING"

_____." The album was recorded at the famous Santa Barbara
NOUN

_____ Festival by the _____ Rock Band,
NOUN   PERSON IN ROOM (MALE)

featuring the super-_____ guitars. Act now! This may be your last
ADJECTIVE

chance to get such a/an _____ bargain.
ADJECTIVE

MAD LIBS® is fun to play with friends, but you can also play it by yourself! To begin with, DO NOT look at the story on the page below. Fill in the blanks on this page with the words called for. Then, using the words you have selected, fill in the blank spaces in the story.

Now you've created your own hilarious MAD LIBS® game!

THE ADVENTURES OF

JANE _____
EXCLAMATION

EXCLAMATION _____

SAME EXCLAMATION _____

ADJECTIVE _____

OCCUPATION _____

OCCUPATION _____

PLURAL NOUN _____

VERB _____

SILLY WORD _____

PLURAL NOUN _____

ADJECTIVE _____

COLOR _____

ARTICLE OF CLOTHING _____

PART OF THE BODY _____

NOUN _____

ARTICLE OF CLOTHING _____

NOUN _____

VERB _____

MAD LIBS®
THE ADVENTURES OF JANE _____
EXCLAMATION

Jane _____ is a great comic book. It's the story of _____
    SAME EXCLAMATION   ADJECTIVE

Jane Jones, who is a/an _____ by day, but sneaks around the
                         OCCUPATION

city by night as a/an _____. Jane is asked by a group of
                      OCCUPATION

_____ to help them _____ and protect the
PLURAL NOUN   VERB

planet from the _____ Armada, who are going to attack the
                  SILLY WORD

planet and destroy all the _____! Jane has some of the most
                    PLURAL NOUN

_____ gadgets around. She wears a/an _____
ADJECTIVE   COLOR

_____ on her _____ and carries a rocket-
ARTICLE OF CLOTHING   PART OF THE BODY

powered _____. She even has a/an _____ that
        NOUN   ARTICLE OF CLOTHING

turns into a/an _____ at the _____ of a button!
        NOUN   VERB

I think, if I could be any comic-book character at all, I'd want to be Jane,

wouldn't you?

MAD LIBS® is fun to play with friends, but you can also play it by yourself! To begin with, DO NOT look at the story on the page below. Fill in the blanks on this page with the words called for. Then, using the words you have selected, fill in the blank spaces in the story.

Now you've created your own hilarious MAD LIBS® game!

JOHNNY COOL, P.I., CHAPTER 1

PERSON IN ROOM (MALE) _____

NOUN _____

NOUN _____

NOUN _____

NOUN _____

NOUN _____

NOUN _____

PART OF THE BODY _____

NOUN _____

NOUN _____

ADJECTIVE _____

ADJECTIVE _____

NOUN _____

NOUN _____

ADVERB _____

MAD LIBS®
JOHNNY COOL, P.I., CHAPTER 1

_____, alias Johnny Cool, hated to make decisions even when
<u>PERSON IN ROOM (MALE)</u>

his _____ depended on it. He headed in the direction of an all-
<u>NOUN</u>

night _____ nestled between a self-service _____
<u>NOUN</u>   <u>NOUN</u>

station and a _____ parlor. He pushed open the diner
<u>NOUN</u>

_____ but didn't enter. The only streetlamp on the dark
<u>NOUN</u>

_____ illuminated the fear on his _____.
<u>NOUN</u>   <u>PART OF THE BODY</u>

He was coming to another decisive moment, and as always, it scared the

_____ out of him. He took a deep _____
<u>NOUN</u>   <u>NOUN</u>

and entered the diner. It was almost _____. Johnny
<u>ADJECTIVE</u>

slumped into a/an _____ leather booth. He was tired. Every
<u>ADJECTIVE</u>

_____ in his body ached. His _____ was trembling.
<u>NOUN</u>   <u>NOUN</u>

He needed coffee _____.
<u>ADVERB</u>

MAD LIBS® is fun to play with friends, but you can also play it by yourself! To begin with, DO NOT look at the story on the page below. Fill in the blanks on this page with the words called for. Then, using the words you have selected, fill in the blank spaces in the story.

Now you've created your own hilarious MAD LIBS® game!

JOHNNY COOL, P.I., CHAPTER 2

PLURAL NOUN _____

NOUN _____

COLOR _____

TYPE OF LIQUID _____

NOUN _____

VERB (PAST TENSE) _____

NOUN _____

NOUN _____

NOUN _____

PART OF THE BODY _____

ADJECTIVE _____

NOUN _____

PLURAL NOUN _____

NOUN _____

VERB ENDING IN "ING" _____

Johnny Cool drummed his _____ on the _____
                              PLURAL NOUN   NOUN

in the restaurant. The _____-haired waitress brought him a cup of
                              COLOR

steaming, hot _____ and a grease-splattered _____.
                    TYPE OF LIQUID   NOUN

He _____ at the menu. The moment he'd been dreading had come.
        VERB (PAST TENSE)

Shivers ran up and down his _____. Beads of _____
                                      NOUN   NOUN

poured over his _____ and down his _____.
                        NOUN   PART OF THE BODY

"Made up your mind?" asked the _____ waitress. Johnny reached
                                        ADJECTIVE

for his voice, and in a barely audible _____, said, "Ham and
                                                NOUN

scrambled _____." "Okay," said the waitress, writing it down on
                PLURAL NOUN

her _____. "What kind of toast would you like—white or
          NOUN

wheat?" Johnny Cool could not handle another decision. He ran out of the diner

_____ at the top of his lungs.
VERB ENDING IN "ING"

MAD LIBS® is fun to play with friends, but you can also play it by yourself! To begin with, DO NOT look at the story on the page below. Fill in the blanks on this page with the words called for. Then, using the words you have selected, fill in the blank spaces in the story.

Now you've created your own hilarious MAD LIBS® game!

CAMPING TRIP

NOUN _____

PLURAL NOUN _____

ADJECTIVE _____

ADJECTIVE _____

ADJECTIVE _____

NOUN _____

PART OF THE BODY (PLURAL) _____

ADJECTIVE _____

VERB (PAST TENSE) _____

ADJECTIVE _____

ADJECTIVE _____

EXCLAMATION _____

ADJECTIVE _____

ADJECTIVE _____

ADJECTIVE _____

MAD LIBS®
CAMPING TRIP

A group of us were sitting around a raging _____ one night
                                              NOUN

roasting _____ and telling _____ stories when we heard
          PLURAL NOUN   ADJECTIVE

a/an _____ noise coming right from the fire. We jumped up and
      ADJECTIVE

saw a/an _____ light floating toward us. It looked like a disembodied
          ADJECTIVE

_____, and we had to cover our _____ because
    NOUN   PART OF THE BODY (PLURAL)

it was so _____. The weird figure _____ above
            ADJECTIVE   VERB (PAST TENSE)

the flames until the fire went out, leaving us in total _____-ness.
                                                          ADJECTIVE

Then, as quickly as it had arrived, the _____ apparition
                                          ADJECTIVE

drifted away and—_____ and behold—the fire was raging
                    EXCLAMATION

again. In addition, all our _____ food had disappeared. Nobody
                              ADJECTIVE

believed this story when we got home, but we decided that whatever the

_____ thing was, it didn't want us to eat all the
    ADJECTIVE

_____ marshmallows.
    ADJECTIVE

MAD LIBS® is fun to play with friends, but you can also play it by yourself! To begin with, DO NOT look at the story on the page below. Fill in the blanks on this page with the words called for. Then, using the words you have selected, fill in the blank spaces in the story.

Now you've created your own hilarious MAD LIBS® game!

DIALOGUE BETWEEN TOURIST AND SALESPERSON

PERSON IN ROOM (MALE) _____

PERSON IN ROOM (FEMALE) _____

PLURAL NOUN _____

PLURAL NOUN _____

A PLACE _____

ADJECTIVE _____

NOUN _____

PLURAL NOUN _____

ADJECTIVE _____

A PLACE _____

NOUN _____

COLOR _____

NOUN _____

NOUN _____

NUMBER _____

ADJECTIVE _____

MAD LIBS®
DIALOGUE BETWEEN TOURIST AND SALESPERSON

Played by _____ *and* _____.
      PERSON IN ROOM (MALE)   PERSON IN ROOM (FEMALE)

BOY: Hello there, Miss. I am looking for some postal _____ that I
                                                        PLURAL NOUN

can mail back to my _____ in (the) _____.
                        PLURAL NOUN   A PLACE

GIRL: We have some very _____ cards. Would you like some with
                              ADJECTIVE

pictures of our local _____ or with pictures of _____
                            NOUN   PLURAL NOUN

growing along the beach?

BOY: I would like five of those that show my _____ hotel.
                                                    ADJECTIVE

GIRL: All right. Now, how about this bumper sticker that says "(the)

_____, America's greatest little _____"?
   A PLACE   NOUN

BOY: No, thanks. But I would like to see one of those _____ hats
                                                            COLOR

with the _____ on top.
              NOUN

GIRL: Okay. Here. My, you look just like a/an _____.
                                                    NOUN

BOY: Good. I'll take it. Now if you can sell me some _____-cent
                                                          NUMBER

stamps, I'll let all my friends back home know what a/an _____
                                                              ADJECTIVE

time I'm having.

MAD LIBS® is fun to play with friends, but you can also play it by yourself! To begin with, DO NOT look at the story on the page below. Fill in the blanks on this page with the words called for. Then, using the words you have selected, fill in the blank spaces in the story.

Now you've created your own hilarious MAD LIBS® game!

PHOTOGRAPHY

PLURAL NOUN _____

PLURAL NOUN _____

ADJECTIVE _____

ADJECTIVE _____

PERSON IN ROOM _____

PLURAL NOUN _____

NOUN _____

NOUN _____

NOUN _____

VERB _____

PART OF THE BODY _____

VERB ENDING IN "ING" _____

VERB _____

TYPE OF FOOD _____

ADJECTIVE _____

ADJECTIVE _____

MAD LIBS®
PHOTOGRAPHY

With today's automatic cameras and their built-in _____ and
PLURAL NOUN

zoom _____, even a/an _____ amateur can take a/an
PLURAL NOUN   ADJECTIVE

_____ picture. Here are a few tips from _____,
ADJECTIVE   PERSON IN ROOM

one of the world's greatest _____.
PLURAL NOUN

Never load _____ into your camera in direct _____-light.
NOUN   NOUN

Make sure you remove the lens _____ before you _____
NOUN   VERB

a picture.

Be careful not to put your _____ in front of the lens when
PART OF THE BODY

_____ a picture.
VERB ENDING IN "ING"

For portraits, have your subject _____ and say, "_____!"
VERB   TYPE OF FOOD

Follow this _____ advice, and in no time at all you should be a/an
ADJECTIVE

_____ photographer.
ADJECTIVE

MAD LIBS® is fun to play with friends, but you can also play it by yourself! To begin with, DO NOT look at the story on the page below. Fill in the blanks on this page with the words called for. Then, using the words you have selected, fill in the blank spaces in the story.

Now you've created your own hilarious MAD LIBS® game!

YOU'RE INVITED

PERSON IN ROOM (FEMALE) _____

ADJECTIVE _____

NOUN _____

NOUN _____

CELEBRITY _____

ADVERB _____

NUMBER _____

ADJECTIVE _____

NOUN _____

NOUN _____

PART OF THE BODY _____

PLURAL NOUN _____

ADJECTIVE _____

PLURAL NOUN _____

PLURAL NOUN _____

ADJECTIVE _____

PLURAL NOUN _____

LETTER OF THE ALPHABET _____

CELEBRITY _____

SAME CELEBRITY _____

ADJECTIVE _____

MAD LIBS®
YOU'RE INVITED

Dear _____,
PERSON IN ROOM (FEMALE)

I would like to invite you to a/an _____ sleepover party this
ADJECTIVE

Friday night at my _____. I live on the corner of South
NOUN

_____ Street and _____ Lane. Please arrive
NOUN   CELEBRITY

_____ at _____ o'clock. Don't forget to bring
ADVERB   NUMBER

a/an _____ sleeping _____ and a soft
ADJECTIVE   NOUN

_____ to rest your _____ on. We'll
NOUN   PART OF THE BODY

have pizza topped with _____ for dinner, and we'll watch
PLURAL NOUN

a/an _____ movie. When it is time for bed, we'll all change
ADJECTIVE

into our _____ and turn out the _____. Then
PLURAL NOUN   PLURAL NOUN

we'll tell _____ ghost stories and talk about all the cute
ADJECTIVE

_____ at school! Please RSV-_____ to me
PLURAL NOUN   LETTER OF THE ALPHABET

by e-mail at iluv-_____@_____.com. Hope you
CELEBRITY   SAME CELEBRITY

can join our _____ party!
ADJECTIVE

MAD LIBS® is fun to play with friends, but you can also play it by yourself! To begin with, DO NOT look at the story on the page below. Fill in the blanks on this page with the words called for. Then, using the words you have selected, fill in the blank spaces in the story.

Now you've created your own hilarious MAD LIBS® game!

CAR TRIP TRAVAILS

ADJECTIVE _____

PLURAL NOUN _____

NOUN _____

ADJECTIVE _____

ADJECTIVE _____

PART OF THE BODY (PLURAL) _____

NOUN _____

NOUN _____

NUMBER _____

PERSON IN ROOM (MALE) _____

PERSON IN ROOM (FEMALE) _____

PLURAL NOUN _____

ADJECTIVE _____

ADJECTIVE _____

PART OF THE BODY (PLURAL) _____

NOUN _____

NOUN _____

NOUN _____

MAD LIBS®
CAR TRIP TRAVAILS

Based on many _____ past experiences, this family should never
ADJECTIVE

take car _____—certainly not together. The last time the
PLURAL NOUN

seven of us were all in one _____, there were three
NOUN

_____ arguments, a/an _____ fistfight,
ADJECTIVE   ADJECTIVE

and a couple of bloody _____—and that was just on the
PART OF THE BODY (PLURAL)

drive to the local super-_____. Recently, we were on our way
NOUN

to Grandma and Grandpa's _____, which is at least a/an
NOUN

_____-hour drive away. Dad was pulling out of the driveway
NUMBER

when my brother _____ and sister _____
PERSON IN ROOM (MALE)   PERSON IN ROOM (FEMALE)

started to argue about who would read the Mad _____ and
PLURAL NOUN

who would fill in the _____ blanks. Dad brought the car to a/an
ADJECTIVE

_____ stop. He was so angry, smoke seemed to be coming out of
ADJECTIVE

his _____. "One more _____ out of any of you
PART OF THE BODY (PLURAL)   NOUN

and this _____ is over," he snapped. "Now, any questions?" Our kid
NOUN

brother timidly raised his _____ and asked, "Are we there yet?"
NOUN

MAD LIBS® is fun to play with friends, but you can also play it by yourself! To begin with, DO NOT look at the story on the page below. Fill in the blanks on this page with the words called for. Then, using the words you have selected, fill in the blank spaces in the story.

Now you've created your own hilarious MAD LIBS® game!

FIVE TIPS FOR A PERFECT WEDDING

ADJECTIVE _____

NOUN _____

NOUN _____

NOUN _____

NOUN _____

NOUN _____

ADJECTIVE _____

PLURAL NOUN _____

PLURAL NOUN _____

COLOR _____

PLURAL NOUN _____

COLOR _____

PLURAL NOUN _____

NUMBER _____

NUMBER _____

PLURAL NOUN _____

PLURAL NOUN _____

VERB _____

NOUN _____

NOUN _____

ADJECTIVE _____

MAD LIBS®
FIVE TIPS FOR A PERFECT WEDDING

The bride should always wear a/an _____ _____,
                                        ADJECTIVE   NOUN

the groom a/an _____.
                     NOUN

The bride's _____ should always pay for the _____,
                  NOUN   NOUN

while the _____ of the groom should pick up the tab for the
                 NOUN

_____ dinner the night before the wedding.
   ADJECTIVE

One color scheme should be followed when choosing the _____
                                                            PLURAL NOUN

as well as the _____. For example, if you choose _____
                   PLURAL NOUN   COLOR

_____, then you should have _____ _____.
   PLURAL NOUN   COLOR   PLURAL NOUN

The bride should choose _____ to _____ of her
                              NUMBER   NUMBER

closest _____ to be her attendants. The groom should choose the
            PLURAL NOUN

same number of his _____ to be the groomsmen.
                         PLURAL NOUN

Guests should remember to _____ on time. Remember, it's the
                                VERB

_____ and _____'s _____ day, and
     NOUN   NOUN   ADJECTIVE

you don't want to ruin it!

MAD LIBS® is fun to play with friends, but you can also play it by yourself! To begin with, DO NOT look at the story on the page below. Fill in the blanks on this page with the words called for. Then, using the words you have selected, fill in the blank spaces in the story.

Now you've created your own hilarious MAD LIBS® game!

SOME OUTER SPACE POETRY

NOUN _____

NOUN _____

NOUN _____

ANIMAL _____

NOUN _____

NOUN _____

VERB (PAST TENSE) _____

NOUN _____

NOUN _____

NOUN _____

VERB (PAST TENSE) _____

Twinkle, twinkle little _____,
NOUN

How I wonder what you are.

Up above the _____ so high,
NOUN

Just like a/an _____ in the sky.
NOUN

Hey diddle diddle, the _____
ANIMAL

And the _____,
NOUN

The cow jumped over the _____.
NOUN

The little dog _____ to see such sport,
VERB (PAST TENSE)

And the _____ ran away with the spoon.
NOUN

Star light, star bright, first _____ I see tonight.
NOUN

I wish I may, I wish I might,

Have the _____ I _____ tonight.
NOUN   VERB (PAST TENSE)

MAD LIBS® is fun to play with friends, but you can also play it by yourself! To begin with, DO NOT look at the story on the page below. Fill in the blanks on this page with the words called for. Then, using the words you have selected, fill in the blank spaces in the story.

Now you've created your own hilarious MAD LIBS® game!

PROM NIGHT, PART 1

PERSON IN ROOM (FEMALE) _____

NOUN _____

ADJECTIVE _____

A PLACE _____

PLURAL NOUN _____

VERB ENDING IN "ING" _____

ADVERB _____

PLURAL NOUN _____

ADJECTIVE _____

SILLY WORD _____

NOUN _____

ADJECTIVE _____

ARTICLE OF CLOTHING (PLURAL) _____

ADJECTIVE _____

ADVERB _____

MAD LIBS®
PROM NIGHT, PART 1

One of the first and finest major horror films of all time was called

_____, about a teenage _____ who was
PERSON IN ROOM (FEMALE)   NOUN

_____. She went to school at (the) _____ and she got good
ADJECTIVE   A PLACE

grades in _____ and _____, but she was always behaving
PLURAL NOUN   VERB ENDING IN "ING"

_____ and did not like her fellow _____. This was
ADVERB   PLURAL NOUN

because they did not like her. They all thought she was _____ and
ADJECTIVE

a/an _____. So at the end of her senior _____,
SILLY WORD   NOUN

this girl was not invited to _____ prom. All of the other students
ADJECTIVE

had dates and new _____ to wear. But they treated their
ARTICLE OF CLOTHING (PLURAL)

classmate as if she were really _____. And she behaved so
ADJECTIVE

_____, it was horrifying.
ADVERB

MAD LIBS® is fun to play with friends, but you can also play it by yourself! To begin with, DO NOT look at the story on the page below. Fill in the blanks on this page with the words called for. Then, using the words you have selected, fill in the blank spaces in the story.

Now you've created your own hilarious MAD LIBS® game!

PROM NIGHT, PART 2

PERSON IN ROOM (FEMALE) _____

PLURAL NOUN _____

NOUN _____

ADJECTIVE _____

PART OF THE BODY _____

PLURAL NOUN _____

VERB ENDING IN "ING" _____

PART OF THE BODY (PLURAL) _____

PLURAL NOUN _____

PLURAL NOUN _____

COLOR _____

TYPE OF LIQUID _____

NOUN _____

VERB ENDING IN "ING" _____

VERB ENDING IN "ING" _____

NOUN _____

VERB ENDING IN "ING" _____

EXCLAMATION _____

SAME PERSON IN ROOM (FEMALE)_____

MAD LIBS®

PROM NIGHT, PART 2

_____ was so mad at all of the other _____ at
PERSON IN ROOM (FEMALE)   PLURAL NOUN

her school that she decided to ruin their _____. You see, she
NOUN

had _____ magical powers and if she concentrated on her
ADJECTIVE

_____, she could start fires or make _____ start
PART OF THE BODY   PLURAL NOUN

_____. So she went to the place where the dance was being
VERB ENDING IN "ING"

held and her _____ blazed out magical energy and all
PART OF THE BODY (PLURAL)

of the girls' _____ burst into _____.
PLURAL NOUN   PLURAL NOUN

Then _____ _____ began dripping from the
COLOR   TYPE OF LIQUID

_____ all over everyone. At this point, everyone began
NOUN

_____ and _____ and trying to get
VERB ENDING IN "ING"   VERB ENDING IN "ING"

out, but there was only one little _____. The students were
NOUN

_____ on one another and screaming, "_____!"
VERB ENDING IN "ING"   EXCLAMATION

It really taught those students a lesson. The lesson was, "Don't forget to invite

_____."
SAME PERSON IN ROOM (FEMALE)

MAD LIBS® is fun to play with friends, but you can also play it by yourself! To begin with, DO NOT look at the story on the page below. Fill in the blanks on this page with the words called for. Then, using the words you have selected, fill in the blank spaces in the story.

Now you've created your own hilarious MAD LIBS® game!

RECIPE FOR AN UPSIDE-DOWN CAKE

ADJECTIVE _____

NOUN _____

NOUN _____

NUMBER _____

NOUN _____

ADJECTIVE _____

ADJECTIVE _____

ADJECTIVE _____

VERB _____

NOUN _____

ADVERB _____

PLURAL NOUN _____

NOUN _____

NOUN _____

VERB _____

NOUN _____

ADJECTIVE _____

VERB (PAST TENSE) _____

NOUN _____

MAD LIBS®
RECIPE FOR AN UPSIDE-DOWN CAKE

Here is a/an _____ recipe for an Upside-Down _____ .
ADJECTIVE   NOUN

First, you preheat your _____ to _____ degrees. Then
NOUN   NUMBER

take a stick of _____ and melt it in a ten-inch _____
NOUN   ADJECTIVE

skillet over a very _____ flame. In a/an _____
ADJECTIVE   ADJECTIVE

bowl _____ granulated _____ and flour, stirring
VERB   NOUN

the mixture _____. Add milk and _____ and beat
ADVERB   PLURAL NOUN

rapidly with an electric _____. Bake until your _____
NOUN   NOUN

is ready. After the cake cools, _____ it from the _____
VERB   NOUN

and turn it upside _____. Serve the cake warm with
ADJECTIVE

_____ cream of small spoonfuls of _____ on top.
VERB (PAST TENSE)   NOUN

MAD LIBS® is fun to play with friends, but you can also play it by yourself! To begin with, DO NOT look at the story on the page below. Fill in the blanks on this page with the words called for. Then, using the words you have selected, fill in the blank spaces in the story.

Now you've created your own hilarious MAD LIBS® game!

STRIKE THREE, YOU'RE OUT!

NOUN _____

NOUN _____

NOUN _____

ADJECTIVE _____

NOUN _____

NOUN _____

NOUN _____

ADJECTIVE _____

NOUN _____

NOUN _____

NOUN _____

NOUN _____

ADJECTIVE _____

NOUN _____

ADJECTIVE _____

ANIMAL (PLURAL) _____

MAD LIBS®
STRIKE THREE, YOU'RE OUT!

If you are sitting in a ball _____ and you hear fans yelling, "Get rid
NOUN

of the _____!" you know they mean the _____. An
NOUN   NOUN

umpire is easy to recognize. He generally wears a/an _____ suit
ADJECTIVE

and has a large, padded _____ to protect his _____.
NOUN   NOUN

At all games, there are four umpires—one at home _____, one
NOUN

at first base, one at second base, and the other at _____ base.
ADJECTIVE

The home plate umpire crouches behind the _____ and decides
NOUN

whether the pitch is a ball or a/an _____. The umpires in the
NOUN

field decide if a player has stolen a/an _____, beat out a/an
NOUN

_____, or whether a fly ball is _____ or foul. An
NOUN   ADJECTIVE

umpire may throw players out of the _____ for calling them
NOUN

_____ names or saying they are as blind as _____.
ADJECTIVE   ANIMAL (PLURAL)

MAD LIBS® is fun to play with friends, but you can also play it by yourself! To begin with, DO NOT look at the story on the page below. Fill in the blanks on this page with the words called for. Then, using the words you have selected, fill in the blank spaces in the story.

Now you've created your own hilarious MAD LIBS® game!

NURSERY RHYMES

ADJECTIVE _____

PART OF THE BODY (PLURAL) _____

PART OF THE BODY (PLURAL) _____

ADJECTIVE _____

NOUN _____

VERB _____

TYPE OF LIQUID _____

NOUN _____

VERB ENDING IN "ING" _____

NOUN _____

ADJECTIVE _____

ADJECTIVE _____

PLURAL NOUN _____

PLURAL NOUN _____

NOUN _____

VERB (PAST TENSE) _____

PART OF THE BODY (PLURAL) _____

ADJECTIVE _____

VERB _____

NOUN _____

ADJECTIVE _____

MAD LIBS®
NURSERY RHYMES

When some _____ school students were asked what nursery
ADJECTIVE

rhymes popped into their _____ or were on the tip of their
PART OF THE BODY (PLURAL)

_____, these were their _____ answers:
PART OF THE BODY (PLURAL)   ADJECTIVE

Jack and Jill went up the _____ to _____ a pail of
NOUN   VERB

_____. Jack fell down and broke his _____ and Jill
TYPE OF LIQUID   NOUN

came _____ after.
VERB ENDING IN "ING"

Mary, Mary, quite contrary, how does your _____ grow? With
NOUN

_____ bells and _____ shells and _____
ADJECTIVE   ADJECTIVE   PLURAL NOUN

all in a row.

Three blind _____, see how they run. They all went
PLURAL NOUN

after the _____'s wife, who _____ off their
NOUN   VERB (PAST TENSE)

_____ with a/an _____ knife. Did you
PART OF THE BODY (PLURAL)   ADJECTIVE

ever _____ such a/an _____ in your life as three
VERB   NOUN

_____ mice?
ADJECTIVE

MAD LIBS® is fun to play with friends, but you can also play it by yourself! To begin with, DO NOT look at the story on the page below. Fill in the blanks on this page with the words called for. Then, using the words you have selected, fill in the blank spaces in the story.

Now you've created your own hilarious MAD LIBS® game!

ON DATING A TWIN

NOUN _____

ADVERB _____

PLURAL NOUN _____

PLURAL NOUN _____

PLURAL NOUN _____

PLURAL NOUN _____

PLURAL NOUN _____

NOUN _____

NOUN _____

VERB ENDING IN "ING" _____

PLURAL NOUN _____

PLURAL NOUN _____

PERSON IN ROOM (MALE) _____

PERSON IN ROOM (FEMALE) _____

MAD LIBS®
ON DATING A TWIN

Going out with an identical _____ is _____
NOUN   ADVERB

freaky! No one can tell twins apart, not even their _____ or close
PLURAL NOUN

_____. Everything about them is the same. The color of their
PLURAL NOUN

_____, the shape of their _____, the shape of
PLURAL NOUN   PLURAL NOUN

their chiseled _____, to say nothing of the way they part their
PLURAL NOUN

_____ right down the middle. And when they smile, believe
NOUN

it or not, they have the same _____ in their teeth. They
NOUN

could make things a lot easier by _____ differently. But
VERB ENDING IN "ING"

no, they both wear the same _____ right down to
PLURAL NOUN

their matching _____. I'm telling you, no matter how I try it's
PLURAL NOUN

impossible for me to tell the difference between _____ and
PERON IN ROOM (MALE)

_____.
PERON IN ROOM (FEMALE)

MAD LIBS® is fun to play with friends, but you can also play it by yourself! To begin with, DO NOT look at the story on the page below. Fill in the blanks on this page with the words called for. Then, using the words you have selected, fill in the blank spaces in the story.

Now you've created your own hilarious MAD LIBS® game!

VOTING MADE EASY AS 1, 2, 3

ADJECTIVE _____

PLURAL NOUN _____

NOUN _____

ADVERB _____

VERB ENDING IN "ING" _____

NOUN _____

VERB _____

NOUN _____

NOUN _____

VERB _____

NOUN _____

PART OF THE BODY _____

LETTER OF THE ALPHABET _____

NOUN _____

NOUN _____

EXCLAMATION _____

TYPE OF FOOD _____

VERB _____

NOUN _____

MAD LIBS®
VOTING MADE EASY AS 1, 2, 3

Here are some very _____ instructions on how to vote:

ADJECTIVE

STEP 1: Sign in with one of the _____ at the registration table.

PLURAL NOUN

You may have to show them your _____ to prove your identity.

NOUN

STEP 2: Proceed _____ to an available _____

ADVERB · VERB ENDING IN "ING"

booth. (Be sure to close the _____ behind you so that no one can

NOUN

watch you _____.)

VERB

STEP 3: How you vote varies from _____ to _____.

NOUN · NOUN

In some states, you _____ by pulling a/an _____

VERB · NOUN

with your _____. In others, you must mark a ballot by placing

PART OF THE BODY

a/an _____ in a small _____ opposite your

LETTER OF THE ALPHABET · NOUN

candidate's _____.

NOUN

"_____!" you will cry. "Voting's as easy as _____!"

EXCLAMATION · TYPE OF FOOD

So be sure to _____ on Election Day, because every

VERB

_____ counts!

NOUN

MAD LIBS® is fun to play with friends, but you can also play it by yourself! To begin with, DO NOT look at the story on the page below. Fill in the blanks on this page with the words called for. Then, using the words you have selected, fill in the blank spaces in the story.

Now you've created your own hilarious MAD LIBS® game!

PIRATE PROFILE: BARTHOLOMEW ROBERTS (AKA BLACK BART)

ADJECTIVE _____

NOUN _____

NOUN _____

PERSON IN ROOM _____

ADJECTIVE _____

ADJECTIVE _____

NOUN _____

NOUN _____

ADJECTIVE _____

NOUN _____

NOUN _____

ADJECTIVE _____

ADJECTIVE _____

PART OF THE BODY _____

ADJECTIVE _____

PLURAL NOUN _____

PLURAL NOUN _____

PLURAL NOUN _____

NOUN _____

MAD LIBS®
PIRATE PROFILE: BARTHOLOMEW ROBERTS (AKA BLACK BART)

A/An _____ scholar once said, "You can't judge a/an
          ADJECTIVE

_____ by its _____." According to pirate
          NOUN   NOUN

historian _____, Black Bart, a ruthless and _____
          PERSON IN ROOM   ADJECTIVE

pirate, was a/an _____ example of how looks can be deceiving.
                  ADJECTIVE

Although he was the _____ of a pirate ship, he dressed as if
                     NOUN

he were a/an _____ on the pages of a fashion magazine.
              NOUN

He never went into battle without a/an _____ plume in his
                                        ADJECTIVE

_____, a long-sleeved ruffled _____ tucked into
          NOUN   NOUN

his _____ breeches, and a/an _____ pearl in
     ADJECTIVE   ADJECTIVE

his left _____. Yet in a/an _____ career that
          PART OF THE BODY   ADJECTIVE

spanned a mere two years and six _____, he captured more
                                  PLURAL NOUN

than four hundred sailing _____ and ended up with more than
                           PLURAL NOUN

three hundred million _____ worth of _____.
                       PLURAL NOUN   NOUN

MAD LIBS® is fun to play with friends, but you can also play it by yourself! To begin with, DO NOT look at the story on the page below. Fill in the blanks on this page with the words called for. Then, using the words you have selected, fill in the blank spaces in the story.

Now you've created your own hilarious MAD LIBS® game!

VACATION SPORTS

ADJECTIVE _____

NUMBER _____

PLURAL NOUN _____

ANIMAL _____

NOUN _____

VERB ENDING IN "ING" _____

ADJECTIVE _____

VERB ENDING IN "ING" _____

VERB ENDING IN "ING" _____

NUMBER _____

PLURAL NOUN _____

NUMBER _____

NOUN _____

NOUN _____

NOUN _____

ADVERB _____

MAD LIBS®
VACATION SPORTS

There are many new and _____ things you can do on your
ADJECTIVE

vacation today. _____ years ago, _____ who
NUMBER   PLURAL NOUN

went on a vacation could play tennis or go _____-
ANIMAL

back riding, or play eighteen holes of _____, or spend
NOUN

their time _____ with their family. But today, if you are
VERB ENDING IN "ING"

_____ enough to try, you can go skydiving, or windsurfing, or
ADJECTIVE

water-skiing, or mountain _____. Skydiving is the most
VERB ENDING IN "ING"

fun, if you are not afraid of _____. First, you strap on
VERB ENDING IN "ING"

_____ parachutes. Then you get in an airplane with eight or nine
NUMBER

other _____ and go up to _____ feet. Then you
PLURAL NOUN   NUMBER

open the door and jump out. Once in the air, everyone holds hands and you go

into a free fall toward the _____ below. At the last minute, you
NOUN

yank on your _____ and open your parachute and float gently to
NOUN

the _____. It is a lot of fun if you like to live _____.
NOUN   ADVERB

MAD LIBS® is fun to play with friends, but you can also play it by yourself! To begin with, DO NOT look at the story on the page below. Fill in the blanks on this page with the words called for. Then, using the words you have selected, fill in the blank spaces in the story.

Now you've created your own hilarious MAD LIBS® game!

TYRANNOSAURUS REX

PLURAL NOUN _____

ADJECTIVE _____

PLURAL NOUN _____

NOUN _____

PLURAL NOUN _____

PLURAL NOUN _____

ADJECTIVE _____

PLURAL NOUN _____

PLURAL NOUN _____

ADJECTIVE _____

NOUN _____

ADJECTIVE _____

PLURAL NOUN _____

PLURAL NOUN _____

NOUN _____

Dinosaur bones and _____ have been discovered from a period
                     PLURAL NOUN

known as the _____ Age. From these fossils, scientists learned
                  ADJECTIVE

that dinosaurs were the largest _____ that ever inhabited the
                                    PLURAL NOUN

_____. The fiercest by far was Tyrannosaurus rex, who ruled the
       NOUN

land at the same time that the flying _____ ruled the skies, and
                                          PLURAL NOUN

the swimming _____ ruled the oceans. These _____
                 PLURAL NOUN   ADJECTIVE

reptiles had serrated _____ for devouring _____.
                          PLURAL NOUN   PLURAL NOUN

With their _____ jaws, they could tear an animal limb from
               ADJECTIVE

_____ with one _____ bite. The world has never
       NOUN   ADJECTIVE

been populated with such ferocious _____, with the possible
                                       PLURAL NOUN

exception of members of the House of _____, who live and work
                                         PLURAL NOUN

in our nation's _____.
                    NOUN

MAD LIBS® is fun to play with friends, but you can also play it by yourself! To begin with, DO NOT look at the story on the page below. Fill in the blanks on this page with the words called for. Then, using the words you have selected, fill in the blank spaces in the story.

Now you've created your own hilarious MAD LIBS® game!

DESCRIPTION OF THE LOVELY GROUP THAT I AM IN

ADJECTIVE _____

ADJECTIVE _____

PERSON IN ROOM _____

ADVERB _____

PLURAL NOUN _____

NUMBER _____

ADJECTIVE _____

ADVERB _____

PERSON IN ROOM _____

ADJECTIVE _____

NOUN _____

PERSON IN ROOM _____

NOUN _____

ADJECTIVE _____

ADJECTIVE _____

ADJECTIVE _____

MAD⊙LIBS®
DESCRIPTION OF THE LOVELY GROUP THAT I AM IN

We are having a perfectly _____ time this evening in the
                                    ADJECTIVE

_____ home of _____. The rooms are decorated
        ADJECTIVE   PERSON IN ROOM

_____ with many stylish _____ that must have
        ADVERB   PLURAL NOUN

cost at least _____ dollars. The guests are all _____
                    NUMBER   ADJECTIVE

conversationalists and are all _____ dressed. _____
                                        ADVERB   PERSON IN ROOM

has been entertaining us by telling us about the time he/she showed his/her

_____ _____ to _____, who
        ADJECTIVE   NOUN   PERSON IN ROOM

mistook it for an early American _____. The refreshments are
                                            NOUN

_____, and the idea of serving hot and _____ hors
        ADJECTIVE   ADJECTIVE

d'oeuvres showed imagination. Visiting here is always a/an _____
                                                                    ADJECTIVE

experience!

MAD LIBS® is fun to play with friends, but you can also play it by yourself! To begin with, DO NOT look at the story on the page below. Fill in the blanks on this page with the words called for. Then, using the words you have selected, fill in the blank spaces in the story.

Now you've created your own hilarious MAD LIBS® game!

SPECIALTY OF THE HOUSE

PERSON IN ROOM _____

VERB ENDING IN "ING" _____

PART OF THE BODY _____

ANIMAL _____

NOUN _____

NUMBER _____

PLURAL NOUN _____

NOUN _____

VERB (PAST TENSE) _____

TYPE OF FOOD _____

TYPE OF LIQUID _____

ADJECTIVE _____

COLOR _____

NOUN _____

PLURAL NOUN _____

NUMBER _____

COLOR _____

PLURAL NOUN _____

NOUN _____

MAD LIBS®
SPECIALTY OF THE HOUSE

Here is Chef _____ 's award-_____
               PERSON IN ROOM   VERB ENDING IN "ING"

recipe for roast _____ of _____ : Choose a
                   PART OF THE BODY   ANIMAL

_____ weighing about _____ _____.
       NOUN   NUMBER   PLURAL NOUN

Remove excess _____ . Add five cloves of garlic, peeled
                      NOUN

and _____ . Season with two tablespoons of chopped
         VERB (PAST TENSE)

_____ . Add a tablespoon of _____ . Sprinkle with a
    TYPE OF FOOD   TYPE OF LIQUID

touch of _____ salt. Add a pinch of ground _____
          ADJECTIVE   COLOR

_____ . Cook at 350 _____ for _____
   NOUN   PLURAL NOUN   NUMBER

minutes. Remove from the oven when the skin is _____ . Serve
                                        COLOR

with mashed _____ and a/an _____ .
        PLURAL NOUN   NOUN

MAD LIBS® is fun to play with friends, but you can also play it by yourself! To begin with, DO NOT look at the story on the page below. Fill in the blanks on this page with the words called for. Then, using the words you have selected, fill in the blank spaces in the story.

Now you've created your own hilarious MAD LIBS® game!

THE GLEAMING

PERSON IN ROOM _____

NOUN _____

NOUN _____

ADJECTIVE _____

NOUN _____

NOUN _____

ADVERB _____

NUMBER _____

ADJECTIVE _____

ADJECTIVE _____

NOUN _____

ADJECTIVE _____

OCCUPATION _____

PART OF THE BODY _____

ADVERB _____

VERB ENDING IN "ING" _____

VERB ENDING IN "ING" _____

VERB (PAST TENSE) _____

ANIMAL _____

MAD LIBS®
THE GLEAMING

One of _____'s first big roles was playing the part of the
___PERSON IN ROOM___

_____ in the horror classic called *The Gleaming* _____.
___NOUN___   ___NOUN___

This _____ movie tells the story of a writer who needs a quiet
___ADJECTIVE___

place to work, so he rents a/an _____ in Colorado in the middle of
___NOUN___

winter. He takes his wife and small _____ with him. Then it snows
___NOUN___

_____ for _____ days, and the couple discovers the
___ADVERB___   ___NUMBER___

_____ place is haunted by the ghost of a/an _____
___ADJECTIVE___   ___ADJECTIVE___

_____. Well, this _____ ghost is the evil spirit of
___NOUN___   ___ADJECTIVE___

a former _____ in the Revolutionary Army. It takes possession of his
___OCCUPATION___

_____ and forces him to act _____ toward
___PART OF THE BODY___   ___ADVERB___

his own son. At this point, there is a lot of _____ and
___VERB ENDING IN "ING"___

_____, but before he can harm anyone he is _____
___VERB ENDING IN "ING"___   ___VERB (PAST TENSE)___

by a stray _____.
___ANIMAL___

MAD LIBS® is fun to play with friends, but you can also play it by yourself! To begin with, DO NOT look at the story on the page below. Fill in the blanks on this page with the words called for. Then, using the words you have selected, fill in the blank spaces in the story.

Now you've created your own hilarious MAD LIBS® game!

ON THE DAY I WAS BORN

ADJECTIVE _____

ADJECTIVE _____

NOUN _____

A PLACE _____

VERB ENDING IN "ING" _____

NOUN _____

VERB (PAST TENSE) _____

NOUN _____

ADJECTIVE _____

NUMBER _____

NUMBER _____

ADJECTIVE _____

NOUN _____

ADJECTIVE _____

ADJECTIVE _____

MAD LIBS®

ON THE DAY I WAS BORN

My mother loves to tell the ____________________ story of the day I was
ADJECTIVE

born. She says it was the most _______________ day of her life. Mom woke
ADJECTIVE

up in the middle of the ______________, and my dad rushed her to (the)
NOUN

______________. When I was born, I immediately began __________________
A PLACE — VERB ENDING IN "ING"

and crying, and the doctor announced, "It's a/an __________________!" My
NOUN

parents _____________________ with joy. The doctor wrapped me in a soft
VERB (PAST TENSE)

_____________________ and handed me to my __________________ mom. I
NOUN — ADJECTIVE

weighed just __________________ pounds and __________________ ounces.
NUMBER — NUMBER

Mom called me her ____________________ bundle of __________________ and
ADJECTIVE — NOUN

said I was the most __________________ thing she had ever seen. (But I've seen
ADJECTIVE

the pictures, and I think I looked like a/an __________________ blob!)
ADJECTIVE

MAD LIBS® is fun to play with friends, but you can also play it by yourself! To begin with, DO NOT look at the story on the page below. Fill in the blanks on this page with the words called for. Then, using the words you have selected, fill in the blank spaces in the story.

Now you've created your own hilarious MAD LIBS® game!

COOKING WITH CHEF _____
FIRST NAME

FIRST NAME _____

VERB _____

ADJECTIVE _____

ADJECTIVE _____

TYPE OF LIQUID _____

ADJECTIVE _____

NUMBER _____

ADJECTIVE _____

PLURAL NOUN _____

VERB _____

ADJECTIVE _____

ADJECTIVE _____

NOUN _____

TYPE OF FOOD (PLURAL) _____

NOUN _____

ADJECTIVE _____

NOUN _____

NOUN _____

PART OF THE BODY _____

MAD LIBS®

COOKING WITH CHEF_____
FIRST NAME

You know what we're going to _____ today? A/An _____
                                VERB   ADJECTIVE

favorite of mine—a crab salad with fennel and _____ onions. To
                                                ADJECTIVE

speed things along, I've already boiled a gallon of _____, added
                                                    TYPE OF LIQUID

¼ cup of _____ salt, and dropped in the crabs and cooked them
         ADJECTIVE

for _____ minutes. Now that they are _____, I will
    NUMBER   ADJECTIVE

crack them into little _____. Next we have to _____
                       PLURAL NOUN   VERB

the onions and the fennel until they are _____. To make the
                                          ADJECTIVE

salad, we put the _____ crabs into a large _____
                  ADJECTIVE   NOUN

and add the fennel, the onion, and a hefty portion of _____. To
                                                      TYPE OF FOOD (PLURAL)

dress the salad, sprinkle it with _____ oil, a touch of _____
                                  NOUN   ADJECTIVE

lemon juice, and a pinch of _____ and pepper. Okay, let's toss this
                            NOUN

_____ and taste it. Yum . . . delicious! A winner! A salad guaranteed
NOUN

to make your _____ water!
             PART OF THE BODY

MAD LIBS® is fun to play with friends, but you can also play it by yourself! To begin with, DO NOT look at the story on the page below. Fill in the blanks on this page with the words called for. Then, using the words you have selected, fill in the blank spaces in the story.

Now you've created your own hilarious MAD LIBS® game!

A WINTER GAME BROADCAST

CELEBRITY (MALE) _____

NOUN _____

NOUN _____

PLURAL NOUN _____

PLURAL NOUN _____

PERSON IN ROOM (MALE) _____

NOUN _____

NOUN _____

PLURAL NOUN _____

NOUN _____

PLURAL NOUN _____

NOUN _____

ADVERB _____

NOUN _____

PLURAL NOUN _____

ADJECTIVE _____

ADJECTIVE _____

MAD LIBS®
A WINTER GAME BROADCAST

"Hi, we're broadcasting live from the American compound here at the ski village.

Unfortunately, my cohost, _____, has laryngitis and has lost his
CELEBRITY (MALE)

_____. He'll be back with us as soon as his _____
NOUN   NOUN

returns. Now to breaking _____! Sadly, we've learned that less
PLURAL NOUN

than twenty _____ ago, _____, America's best
PLURAL NOUN   PERSON IN ROOM (MALE)

_____ skier and favorite to win the giant slalom, suffered a
NOUN

life-threatening _____ when he plummeted three hundred
NOUN

_____ down the side of a/an _____. According
PLURAL NOUN   NOUN

to the latest hospital _____, he broke his _____,
PLURAL NOUN   NOUN

but doctors are hopeful he'll heal _____ and be back on his
ADVERB

_____ by the end of the year. Our fervent _____
NOUN   PLURAL NOUN

go out to this _____ skier and his entire _____ family."
ADJECTIVE   ADJECTIVE

MAD LIBS® is fun to play with friends, but you can also play it by yourself! To begin with, DO NOT look at the story on the page below. Fill in the blanks on this page with the words called for. Then, using the words you have selected, fill in the blank spaces in the story.

Now you've created your own hilarious MAD LIBS® game!

THANK-YOU LETTERS

PERSON IN ROOM (FEMALE) _____

ADJECTIVE _____

NOUN _____

PLURAL NOUN _____

PART OF THE BODY _____

ADJECTIVE _____

ADJECTIVE _____

PERSON IN ROOM (MALE) _____

NOUN _____

PLURAL NOUN _____

ADJECTIVE _____

PLURAL NOUN _____

ADJECTIVE _____

PLURAL NOUN _____

NOUN _____

CELEBRITY _____

MAD LIBS®
THANK-YOU LETTERS

Dear Auntie _____,
　　　　　　　PERSON IN ROOM (FEMALE)

I want to thank you for sending me the _____ gift. I never had a/an
　　　　　　　　　　　　　　　　　　　　　　ADJECTIVE

_____ before. I can use it to fix all my _____. It
NOUN　　　　　　　　　　　　　　　　　　　　　　PLURAL NOUN

will also keep my _____ warm if we have any _____
　　　　　　　　　PART OF THE BODY　　　　　　　　　　　　ADJECTIVE

weather.

　　　Your _____ nephew,
　　　　　　　ADJECTIVE

_____
　　PERSON IN ROOM (MALE)

Dear Grandpa and Grandma,

I really like the _____ you sent me. It must have cost a lot
　　　　　　　　　NOUN

of _____. All of the kids around here have _____
　　PLURAL NOUN　　　　　　　　　　　　　　　　　　　　ADJECTIVE

computers. But mine is the only one that has six different _____.
　　　　　　　　　　　　　　　　　　　　　　　　　　　PLURAL NOUN

It will help me do my _____ homework, and I know I will
　　　　　　　　　　ADJECTIVE

get higher _____ this year. Mom says I can come to your
　　　　　　PLURAL NOUN

_____ for a visit next summer.
　　NOUN

Signed,

_____
　　CELEBRITY

MAD LIBS® is fun to play with friends, but you can also play it by yourself! To begin with, DO NOT look at the story on the page below. Fill in the blanks on this page with the words called for. Then, using the words you have selected, fill in the blank spaces in the story.

Now you've created your own hilarious MAD LIBS® game!

GEORGE WASHINGTON

NOUN _____

ADJECTIVE _____

ADJECTIVE _____

NOUN _____

NOUN _____

EXCLAMATION _____

VERB (PAST TENSE) _____

NOUN _____

NOUN _____

NOUN _____

NOUN _____

NOUN _____

OCCUPATION _____

MAD LIBS®
GEORGE WASHINGTON

George Washington, the father of our _____, was a very

          NOUN

_____ man. When George was a/an _____ boy, he

  ADJECTIVE   ADJECTIVE

took his _____ and chopped down his father's favorite cherry

      NOUN

_____. "_____!" said his father. "Who has

   NOUN   EXCLAMATION

_____ my _____?" Then he saw George holding a

 VERB (PAST TENSE)   NOUN

sharp _____ in his hand. "Father," said George, "I cannot tell a lie.

     NOUN

I did it with my little _____." His father smiled and patted little

              NOUN

George on the _____. "You are a very honest _____,"

        NOUN   NOUN

he said, "and someday you may become the first _____ of the

                            OCCUPATION

United States."

MAD LIBS® is fun to play with friends, but you can also play it by yourself! To begin with, DO NOT look at the story on the page below. Fill in the blanks on this page with the words called for. Then, using the words you have selected, fill in the blank spaces in the story.

Now you've created your own hilarious MAD LIBS® game!

BIRD-WATCHING AND VICE VERSA

PLURAL NOUN _____

ADJECTIVE _____

ADJECTIVE _____

NOUN _____

SILLY WORD _____

VERB _____

NUMBER _____

ADJECTIVE _____

ADJECTIVE _____

PART OF THE BODY _____

PLURAL NOUN _____

NOUN _____

ADJECTIVE _____

NOUN _____

MAD LIBS®
BIRD-WATCHING AND VICE VERSA

Bird-watching can be more fun than a barrel of _____. Our
                                                    PLURAL NOUN

_____ feathered friends are everywhere, waiting to be watched.
        ADJECTIVE

An interesting bird to start with is the _____ oriole, which
                                                    ADJECTIVE

builds its nest in _____ trees. Early in spring, we hear the
                            NOUN

oriole give its mating call, which sounds like this: "_____." Then
                                                                SILLY WORD

the male and female get together and _____. Later, the female lays
                                                    VERB

_____ eggs. Isn't that _____? Another fascinating
        NUMBER   ADJECTIVE

bird is the _____-breasted nuthatch. The nuthatch is very tame.
                    ADJECTIVE

He will fly down and land right on your _____ and eat out of
                                                    PART OF THE BODY

your _____. Other birds to watch out for are the red-crested
            PLURAL NOUN

_____, the _____-necked thrush, and the yellow-
            NOUN   ADJECTIVE

bellied _____ sucker. Now that you know something about birds,
                    NOUN

get out there and watch!

MAD LIBS® is fun to play with friends, but you can also play it by yourself! To begin with, DO NOT look at the story on the page below. Fill in the blanks on this page with the words called for. Then, using the words you have selected, fill in the blank spaces in the story.

Now you've created your own hilarious MAD LIBS® game!

A LETTER WRITTEN BY A LONELY EXTRATERRESTRIAL

PERSON IN ROOM _____

LAST NAME _____

NOUN _____

ADJECTIVE _____

PART OF THE BODY (PLURAL) _____

NOUN _____

NOUN _____

OCCUPATION _____

OCCUPATION _____

EXCLAMATION _____

PART OF THE BODY _____

ADJECTIVE _____

ADVERB _____

A PLACE _____

PLURAL NOUN _____

VERB _____

MAD LIBS®

A LETTER WRITTEN BY A LONELY EXTRATERRESTRIAL

Dear _____,
PERSON IN ROOM

I am writing to you from the planet _____ because I saw
LAST NAME

your picture on the electronic _____, and I think you are very
NOUN

_____. You have the five prettiest _____ I have
ADJECTIVE   PART OF THE BODY (PLURAL)

ever seen. And your _____ is out of this galaxy. I certainly hope
NOUN

that you are a/an _____ of the opposite sex. If you are, and if you
NOUN

aren't a/an _____, then I would like you to be my _____.
OCCUPATION   OCCUPATION

If you read this and your answer is "_____," then I will contact
EXCLAMATION

your father, Darth Vader, and formally ask for your _____. My
PART OF THE BODY

_____ father tells me that two can live as _____
ADJECTIVE   ADVERB

as one, so we can afford to buy a little condo in (the) _____
A PLACE

and settle down and raise some sweet little _____. Please
PLURAL NOUN

_____ to me right away and send a photograph.
VERB

MAD LIBS® is fun to play with friends, but you can also play it by yourself! To begin with, DO NOT look at the story on the page below. Fill in the blanks on this page with the words called for. Then, using the words you have selected, fill in the blank spaces in the story.

Now you've created your own hilarious MAD LIBS® game!

FISHING

NOUN _____

ADJECTIVE _____

VERB _____

NOUN _____

ADVERB _____

ADJECTIVE _____

NOUN _____

NOUN _____

ADJECTIVE _____

NOUN _____

NOUN _____

TYPE OF LIQUID _____

NOUN _____

ADJECTIVE _____

NOUN _____

ADJECTIVE _____

NOUN _____

Fishing is simple. All you need is a fishing _____ and a can of
NOUN

_____ worms. It's easy to tell when you _____ a
ADJECTIVE   VERB

fish. Your float will bob up and down or your _____ will unwind
NOUN

_____. If you want to catch bass, _____ trout, or
ADVERB   ADJECTIVE

wall-eyed _____, you fish in a lake or a mountain _____.
NOUN   NOUN

If it's _____-fin tuna you're after, or a sail-_____,
ADJECTIVE   NOUN

or a sword-_____, you go deep-_____ fishing. This
NOUN   TYPE OF LIQUID

can be expensive. You may have to charter a/an _____ with a
NOUN

captain and a/an _____ mate to sail the _____.
ADJECTIVE   NOUN

Warning! The sea can be very _____ and you could become
ADJECTIVE

_____ sick.
NOUN

MAD LIBS® is fun to play with friends, but you can also play it by yourself! To begin with, DO NOT look at the story on the page below. Fill in the blanks on this page with the words called for. Then, using the words you have selected, fill in the blank spaces in the story.

Now you've created your own hilarious MAD LIBS® game!

CHINESE DINNER

ADJECTIVE _____

ADJECTIVE _____

CELEBRITY _____

ADJECTIVE _____

NOUN _____

ADJECTIVE _____

ADJECTIVE _____

NOUN _____

NOUN _____

TYPE OF FOOD _____

TYPE OF FOOD _____

NOUN _____

TYPE OF FOOD _____

ADJECTIVE _____

MAD LIBS®
CHINESE DINNER

I recently had dinner at a new Chinese restaurant. The cooking was

_____ and the service was _____. The owner
　　　ADJECTIVE　　　　　　　　　　　　　　　　　　ADJECTIVE

of the restaurant, _____, suggested that for my first course I
　　　　　　　　　　　CELEBRITY

have sweet and _____ spare ribs, which is a specialty of the
　　　　　　　　ADJECTIVE

_____. They were _____. For the next course,
　　　NOUN　　　　　　　　　　　　　　ADJECTIVE

I was served a/an _____ _____ soup. The main
　　　　　　　　　ADJECTIVE　　　　　　　　　NOUN

course consisted of egg foo _____, lobster in _____
　　　　　　　　　　　　　　　NOUN　　　　　　　　　　　　　TYPE OF FOOD

sauce, and pressed _____. For dessert, I ordered those famous
　　　　　　　　　TYPE OF FOOD

Chinese _____ cookies with sliced _____. But
　　　　　NOUN　　　　　　　　　　　　　　　　　TYPE OF FOOD

whenever I eat Chinese food, an hour later I feel _____ again.
　　　　　　　　　　　　　　　　　　　　　　　　　ADJECTIVE

MAD LIBS® is fun to play with friends, but you can also play it by yourself! To begin with, DO NOT look at the story on the page below. Fill in the blanks on this page with the words called for. Then, using the words you have selected, fill in the blank spaces in the story.

Now you've created your own hilarious MAD LIBS® game!

TENNIS

ADJECTIVE _____

PLURAL NOUN _____

ADJECTIVE _____

ADJECTIVE _____

PLURAL NOUN _____

NOUN _____

ADJECTIVE _____

NOUN _____

NOUN _____

VERB _____

NOUN _____

ADJECTIVE _____

PART OF THE BODY _____

ADVERB _____

NOUN _____

NOUN _____

EXCLAMATION _____

MAD LIBS®
TENNIS

The most important game you will play at camp is tennis. Tennis is popular

with young people, _____ people, and even with elderly
ADJECTIVE

_____. Playing tennis gets you out in the _____
PLURAL NOUN   ADJECTIVE

air and is really _____ exercise. You can wear special
ADJECTIVE

_____ made especially for the court. The most important part of
PLURAL NOUN

tennis is the serve. To serve, you throw the _____ high in the
NOUN

air and hit it into your opponent's _____ _____.
ADJECTIVE   NOUN

Then you rush up to the _____ and _____. The
NOUN   VERB

various strokes in tennis are called the "overhand _____," the
NOUN

"_____ volley," and the "back- _____ return." And,
ADJECTIVE   PART OF THE BODY

if you win, you must remember to run up and leap _____ over
ADVERB

the _____. Then slap your opponent on the _____
NOUN   NOUN

and say, "_____!"
EXCLAMATION

MAD LIBS® is fun to play with friends, but you can also play it by yourself! To begin with, DO NOT look at the story on the page below. Fill in the blanks on this page with the words called for. Then, using the words you have selected, fill in the blank spaces in the story.

Now you've created your own hilarious MAD LIBS® game!

A RARE MEDIUM

PERSON IN ROOM _____

NOUN _____

NOUN _____

NOUN _____

NOUN _____

ADJECTIVE _____

ADJECTIVE _____

ADJECTIVE _____

NOUN _____

NOUN _____

NOUN _____

VERB _____

ADVERB _____

NOUN _____

ADJECTIVE _____

ADJECTIVE _____

NUMBER _____

NOUN _____

VERB (PAST TENSE) _____

MAD LIBS®
A RARE MEDIUM

The sign read "Madam _____, Have Your _____
                      PERSON IN ROOM   NOUN

Told Today." Taking a deep _____, I opened the _____
                                  NOUN   NOUN

and went inside. In the center of the room, seated behind a large

_____, was the Madam. She was a/an _____
      NOUN   ADJECTIVE

woman with dark _____ eyes and a/an _____ smile
                     ADJECTIVE   ADJECTIVE

on her _____. She was dressed in a large _____
          NOUN   NOUN

and wore a/an _____ wrapped around her head. She motioned
                  NOUN

to me to _____ down as she stared _____ into
          VERB   ADVERB

her crystal _____. A/An _____ look came over her
             NOUN   ADJECTIVE

_____ face. She told me something I didn't want to hear. "If you
  ADJECTIVE

want your fortune told, it's _____ dollars." I leaped out of my
                          NUMBER

_____ and _____ out the door.
  NOUN   VERB (PAST TENSE)

MAD LIBS® is fun to play with friends, but you can also play it by yourself! To begin with, DO NOT look at the story on the page below. Fill in the blanks on this page with the words called for. Then, using the words you have selected, fill in the blank spaces in the story.

Now you've created your own hilarious MAD LIBS® game!

SCIENCE LAB

ADJECTIVE _____

PLURAL NOUN _____

PLURAL NOUN _____

CELEBRITY (FEMALE) _____

PLURAL NOUN _____

PLURAL NOUN _____

PLURAL NOUN _____

ADVERB _____

ADJECTIVE _____

PLURAL NOUN _____

NOUN _____

NOUN _____

ADJECTIVE _____

PERSON IN ROOM _____

NOUN _____

TYPE OF FOOD _____

TYPE OF LIQUID _____

PLURAL NOUN _____

ARTICLE OF CLOTHING (PLURAL) _____

MAD LIBS®
SCIENCE LAB

Once a week, we have a science laboratory class, and we get to do

_____ experiments with _____ and
ADJECTIVE   PLURAL NOUN

_____. Our teacher, Ms. _____, shows us how to
PLURAL NOUN   CELEBRITY (FEMALE)

dissect _____. First, we take out the internal _____
PLURAL NOUN   PLURAL NOUN

and _____ and draw pictures of them in our notebooks. We have
PLURAL NOUN

to work _____ or else we'll make a mess. We also learn to use
ADVERB

chemicals to make _____ things like inexpensive household
ADJECTIVE

_____ and deodorizers that make a/an _____ smell
PLURAL NOUN   NOUN

like a/an _____. Last week, we had a/an _____
NOUN   ADJECTIVE

accident in the lab. _____ mixed some _____ with
PERSON IN ROOM   NOUN

_____ and added some _____ and the mixture
TYPE OF FOOD   TYPE OF LIQUID

exploded and blew two _____ through the roof. So now our
PLURAL NOUN

teacher makes us all wear safety _____ during
ARTICLE OF CLOTHING (PLURAL)

science class.

MAD LIBS® is fun to play with friends, but you can also play it by yourself! To begin with, DO NOT look at the story on the page below. Fill in the blanks on this page with the words called for. Then, using the words you have selected, fill in the blank spaces in the story.

Now you've created your own hilarious MAD LIBS® game!

CLASS PRESIDENT

PLURAL NOUN _____

VERB _____

PLURAL NOUN _____

YEAR _____

VERB (PAST TENSE) _____

NUMBER _____

PLURAL NOUN _____

A PLACE _____

NUMBER _____

ADJECTIVE _____

SILLY WORD _____

NUMBER _____

ADJECTIVE _____

OCCUPATION (PLURAL) _____

ADJECTIVE _____

VERB ENDING IN "ING" _____

ADJECTIVE _____

MAD LIBS®
CLASS PRESIDENT

Good morning, ladies and _____. As your class president, I'd
                              PLURAL NOUN

like to _____ a few _____ about the graduating
              VERB   PLURAL NOUN

class of _____. We've all _____ hard over the
                YEAR   VERB (PAST TENSE)

past _____ years and what a great time we've had! We've
            NUMBER

learned about _____ in (the) _____, and even learned
                 PLURAL NOUN   A PLACE

how to count to _____! That's pretty _____ if you ask
                    NUMBER   ADJECTIVE

me. Especially since we had Mrs. _____ as our teacher for the
                                       SILLY WORD

past _____ years. She was one of the most _____
         NUMBER   ADJECTIVE

_____ we've ever had! I think this year's class is the most
   OCCUPATION (PLURAL)

_____ ever. Although I'm sad to be _____, I know
     ADJECTIVE   VERB ENDING IN "ING"

our graduating class will do _____ things in the future.
                                 ADJECTIVE

MAD LIBS® is fun to play with friends, but you can also play it by yourself! To begin with, DO NOT look at the story on the page below. Fill in the blanks on this page with the words called for. Then, using the words you have selected, fill in the blank spaces in the story.

Now you've created your own hilarious MAD LIBS® game!

HOME VIDEOS

ADJECTIVE _____

NOUN _____

ADJECTIVE _____

ADJECTIVE _____

ADVERB _____

NOUN _____

PART OF THE BODY _____

PART OF THE BODY (PLURAL) _____

PLURAL NOUN _____

ADVERB _____

PLURAL NOUN _____

PLURAL NOUN _____

NOUN _____

NOUN _____

PART OF THE BODY _____

NOUN _____

NUMBER _____

I did it again! Last night we had a/an _____ dinner to celebrate
                                          ADJECTIVE

Mom and Dad's seventeenth wedding _____ and later watch
                                          NOUN

videos of their _____ courtship and _____
                      ADJECTIVE   ADJECTIVE

ceremony. As everyone in the family anticipated, I became _____
                                                                ADVERB

emotional. The moment Dad got down on one _____ and
                                                NOUN

asked Mom for her _____ in marriage, my _____
                      PART OF THE BODY   PART OF THE BODY (PLURAL)

began to tremble and I burst into _____. Okay, I admit it, I'm
                                      PLURAL NOUN

_____ sentimental, but the way Mom and Dad looked into
      ADVERB

each other's _____ when they exchanged their wedding
                  PLURAL NOUN

_____ was a total _____-jerker. They're a match
      PLURAL NOUN   NOUN

made in _____. When the lights came on, there wasn't a dry
              NOUN

_____ in the _____, and I had personally gone
      PART OF THE BODY   NOUN

through _____ packs of tissues.
              NUMBER

MAD LIBS® is fun to play with friends, but you can also play it by yourself! To begin with, DO NOT look at the story on the page below. Fill in the blanks on this page with the words called for. Then, using the words you have selected, fill in the blank spaces in the story.

Now you've created your own hilarious MAD LIBS® game!

LET'S DANCE!

ADJECTIVE _____

PLURAL NOUN _____

NUMBER _____

PLURAL NOUN _____

ADJECTIVE _____

ADVERB _____

ADJECTIVE _____

NOUN _____

VERB (PAST TENSE) _____

PART OF THE BODY _____

PERSON IN ROOM _____

ADJECTIVE _____

NUMBER _____

PART OF THE BODY _____

ADVERB _____

ADJECTIVE _____

PLURAL NOUN _____

ADVERB _____

PLURAL NOUN _____

NOUN _____

PART OF THE BODY (PLURAL) _____

MAD LIBS®
LET'S DANCE!

At my _____ sleepover party, my best _____ and
      ADJECTIVE   PLURAL NOUN

I decided to have a dance-off. We made my _____-year-old little
                                              NUMBER

sister be the judge. We broke into two teams, "The _____" and
                                                         PLURAL NOUN

"The _____ Dancers." My team danced _____, but
        ADJECTIVE   ADVERB

the other team's _____ moves were out of this _____!
                    ADJECTIVE   NOUN

They totally out-_____ us. So when no one was looking, I grabbed
                   VERB (PAST TENSE)

my sister by the _____ and pulled her aside. "_____,"
                  PART OF THE BODY   PERSON IN ROOM

I whispered, "I promise to do all of your _____ chores for
                                             ADJECTIVE

_____ months if you say that my team won." My sister shook
    NUMBER

her _____. "No way!" she said _____. "Your team
     PART OF THE BODY   ADVERB

danced worse than a bunch of _____ _____!"
                                ADJECTIVE   PLURAL NOUN

"Fine," I said. "Then I'll just have to tell all of my friends that you're

_____ afraid of _____." That helped to change her
    ADVERB   PLURAL NOUN

_____. We won that contest, _____ down!
    NOUN   PART OF THE BODY (PLURAL)

MAD LIBS® is fun to play with friends, but you can also play it by yourself! To begin with, DO NOT look at the story on the page below. Fill in the blanks on this page with the words called for. Then, using the words you have selected, fill in the blank spaces in the story.

Now you've created your own hilarious MAD LIBS® game!

ALEXANDER THE GREAT

NOUN _____

NOUN _____

CELEBRITY _____

NOUN _____

CELEBRITY _____

A PLACE _____

NOUN _____

SILLY WORD _____

PLURAL NOUN _____

TYPE OF LIQUID _____

PART OF THE BODY _____

PLURAL NOUN _____

MAD LIBS®
ALEXANDER THE GREAT

In 356 BC, Phillip of Macedonia, the ruler of a province in northern Greece,

became the father of a bouncing baby _____ named Alexander.

NOUN

Alexander's teacher was Aristotle, the famous _____. When he was

NOUN

twenty years old, his father was murdered by _____, after which

CELEBRITY

he became _____ of all Macedonia. In 334, he invaded Persia

NOUN

and defeated _____ at the battle of (the) _____.

CELEBRITY   A PLACE

Later, at Arbela, he won his most important victory, over Darius the Third. This

made him _____ _____ over all Persians. Then

NOUN   SILLY WORD

he marched to India, and many of his _____ died. After that,

PLURAL NOUN

Alexander began drinking too much _____, and at the age of

TYPE OF LIQUID

thirty-three, he died of an infection in the _____. His last words

PART OF THE BODY

are reported to have been, "There are no more _____ to conquer."

PLURAL NOUN

MAD LIBS® is fun to play with friends, but you can also play it by yourself! To begin with, DO NOT look at the story on the page below. Fill in the blanks on this page with the words called for. Then, using the words you have selected, fill in the blank spaces in the story.

Now you've created your own hilarious MAD LIBS® game!

A HEALTH QUIZ

PLURAL NOUN _____

PART OF THE BODY _____

PLURAL NOUN _____

NOUN _____

NOUN _____

NOUN _____

PART OF THE BODY _____

TYPE OF LIQUID _____

NOUN _____

MAD LIBS®
A HEALTH QUIZ

QUESTION: What are germs?

ANSWER: Germs are teensy, tiny little _____. You cannot see them
                                            PLURAL NOUN

with your naked _____. Harmful germs can give you the flu or
                    PART OF THE BODY

the _____.
        PLURAL NOUN

QUESTION: Can you catch a cold by standing in the rain?

ANSWER: If you get wet, it will make your entire _____ weak. If
                                                        NOUN

some germs are in your nose or your _____, you won't be able to
                                            NOUN

fight them. Your _____ will get stuffed up. You can also catch a
                        NOUN

cold if someone coughs or sneezes in your _____.
                                                PART OF THE BODY

QUESTION: How does blood travel around your body?

ANSWER: You have over four quarts of _____ in your body. It is
                                            TYPE OF LIQUID

pumped through your arteries by your _____.
                                            NOUN

MAD LIBS® is fun to play with friends, but you can also play it by yourself! To begin with, DO NOT look at the story on the page below. Fill in the blanks on this page with the words called for. Then, using the words you have selected, fill in the blank spaces in the story.

Now you've created your own hilarious MAD LIBS® game!

THE BIG DANCE

NOUN _____

PERSON IN ROOM (MALE) _____

ADJECTIVE _____

NOUN _____

NOUN _____

NOUN _____

ADJECTIVE _____

COLOR _____

ANIMAL _____

NOUN _____

ADJECTIVE _____

ADJECTIVE _____

MAD LIBS®
THE BIG DANCE

Last night, our school had a big dance to celebrate the _____
                                                                    NOUN

team's homecoming. I went with _____ and some of our
                                PERSON IN ROOM (MALE)

friends. It was really _____. The dance committee went all out and
                        ADJECTIVE

decorated the _____ to look just like a/an _____,
               NOUN   NOUN

with plants, trees, and flowers they bought from a local _____,
                                                          NOUN

and some really _____ sets that were donated by the drama
                 ADJECTIVE

club. There was even a fountain in the middle of the room that was trickling

_____ water into a pool! There was a DJ there—playing all of our
   COLOR

favorite songs. We even danced the _____ Dance! At the end of
                                     ANIMAL

the night, the DJ played "_____ Love," and my _____
                           NOUN   ADJECTIVE

date asked me to dance, even though it was a slow song. It was a/an

_____ night and I'll never forget it!
   ADJECTIVE

MAD LIBS® is fun to play with friends, but you can also play it by yourself! To begin with, DO NOT look at the story on the page below. Fill in the blanks on this page with the words called for. Then, using the words you have selected, fill in the blank spaces in the story.

Now you've created your own hilarious MAD LIBS® game!

AN ADULT WESTERN

LAST NAME _____

ADVERB _____

ADJECTIVE _____

FIRST NAME (MALE) _____

FIRST NAME (FEMALE) _____

ADJECTIVE _____

ADVERB _____

NOUN _____

NOUN _____

NOUN _____

NOUN _____

NOUN _____

NUMBER _____

NOUN _____

TYPE OF LIQUID _____

EXCLAMATION _____

NOUN _____

MAD LIBS

AN ADULT WESTERN

Tex _____, the marshal of Dodge City, rode into town.
　　　　　LAST NAME

He sat _____ in the saddle, ready for trouble. He knew that his
　　　　　ADVERB

_____ enemy, _____ the Kid, was in town.
　　ADJECTIVE　　　　　　　FIRST NAME (MALE)

The Kid was in love with Tex's horse, _____. Suddenly, the Kid
　　　　　　　　　　　　　　　FIRST NAME (FEMALE)

came out of the _____ Nugget Saloon. "Draw, Tex!" he yelled
　　　　　　　ADJECTIVE

_____.
　　ADVERB

Tex reached for his _____, but before he could get it out of his
　　　　　　　　NOUN

_____, the Kid fired twice, hitting Tex in the _____
　　NOUN　　　　　　　　　　　　　　　　　　　　NOUN

and the _____. As Tex fell, he pulled his own _____
　　　　　NOUN　　　　　　　　　　　　　　　　　　NOUN

and shot the Kid _____ times in the _____. The
　　　　　　　　NUMBER　　　　　　　　　　　　NOUN

Kid dropped in a pool of _____.
　　　　　　　　　　　TYPE OF LIQUID

"_____!" Tex said. "I hated to do it, but he was on the wrong side
　　EXCLAMATION

of the _____."
　　　　NOUN

MAD LIBS® is fun to play with friends, but you can also play it by yourself! To begin with, DO NOT look at the story on the page below. Fill in the blanks on this page with the words called for. Then, using the words you have selected, fill in the blank spaces in the story.

Now you've created your own hilarious MAD LIBS® game!

TV CELEBRITY MAGAZINE

PART OF THE BODY _____

FIRST NAME (FEMALE) _____

NOUN _____

NOUN _____

PART OF THE BODY _____

NOUN _____

PLURAL NOUN _____

ADJECTIVE _____

PART OF THE BODY _____

NOUN _____

PLURAL NOUN _____

NOUN _____

ADVERB _____

ADVERB _____

NOUN _____

PART OF THE BODY (PLURAL) _____

Breathless, wearing her glasses on top of her _____,
PART OF THE BODY

_____ rushes into her dressing room on the set of *One*
FIRST NAME (FEMALE)

_____ *to Love*. She's wearing a colorful _____
NOUN   NOUN

around her _____, a full-length _____, and very
PART OF THE BODY   NOUN

cool _____. Offscreen as well as on, she's independent and
PLURAL NOUN

_____ and very comfortable in her own _____.
ADJECTIVE   PART OF THE BODY

You understand immediately why she's a role _____ for
NOUN

millions of teenage _____. Although she's rehearsing her
PLURAL NOUN

_____, she still finds time to _____ talk to us. But before
NOUN   ADVERB

we get far, she's called to the set. The interview ends _____.
ADVERB

Before leaving, she turns and says, "Just because you're thought of as a/an

_____ symbol doesn't mean you don't have a good head on your
NOUN

_____."
PART OF THE BODY (PLURAL)

MAD LIBS® is fun to play with friends, but you can also play it by yourself! To begin with, DO NOT look at the story on the page below. Fill in the blanks on this page with the words called for. Then, using the words you have selected, fill in the blank spaces in the story.

Now you've created your own hilarious MAD LIBS® game!

THE ONE AND ONLY AUNT ROSE

NOUN _____

NOUN _____

NOUN _____

ADJECTIVE _____

SILLY WORD _____

NOUN _____

OCCUPATION _____

PLURAL NOUN _____

NOUN _____

PART OF THE BODY _____

NOUN _____

NOUN _____

ADJECTIVE _____

PLURAL NOUN _____

MAD LIBS®
THE ONE AND ONLY AUNT ROSE

When Aunt Rose was a little _____, she won a/an _____
    NOUN   NOUN

contest reciting a/an _____ and singing her version of "Yankee
                            NOUN

_____ Dandy." From that moment on she was bitten by the acting
  ADJECTIVE

_____. Whenever and wherever there was a casting _____,
  SILLY WORD   NOUN

Aunt Rose would show up and audition for the _____. Like all
                                                    OCCUPATION

actors, she was turned down many, many times, but to her credit it never

dampened her _____. She took rejection with a grain of
                  PLURAL NOUN

_____ and always held her _____ up high.
      NOUN   PART OF THE BODY

But when she had her first child, to the family's surprise, she threw in the

_____ and became a stay-at-home _____. Now
      NOUN   NOUN

whenever Aunt Rose has the urge to perform, she sits at the piano and sings

all the old _____ songs for her grandchildren, nieces, and
                ADJECTIVE

_____.
  PLURAL NOUN

Join the millions of Mad Libs fans creating wacky and wonderful stories on our apps!

Download Mad Libs today!